W0203322

| Gymnasium Bayern |

access 5

WORKBOOK MIT INTERAKTIVEN ÜBUNGEN

Lehrerfassung

Deine **interaktiven Übungen** findest du hier:

1. Melde dich auf scook.de an.
2. Gib den unten stehenden Zugangscode in die Box ein.
3. Hab viel Spaß mit deinen interaktiven Übungen.

Dein Zugangscode auf
www.scook.de

Die interaktiven Übungen können dort nach Bestätigung der allgemeinen Geschäftsbedingungen genutzt werden.

yvmbz-q8yak

Cornelsen

Here we go!

Die interaktive Übung 1 findest du auf www.scook.de. Zum Einloggen auf Scook brauchst du den Code auf Seite 1.

1 Silky and you ➜ SB (p. 9)

Read Silky's sentences. Write your answers.

YOU

1 My name is ______________ .

2 I'm ten/eleven years ______________ old .

3 I 'm ______________ from ______________ .

2 Nina and Dan ➜ SB (p. 9)

Write Nina's questions and Dan's answers.

you · How · are · old? · you · Where · from · are? · your · Hi! · What's · name?

Dan · twelve · Plymouth

1 Hi! What's your name?
2 How old are you?
3 Where are you from?

1 My name is Dan.
2 I'm twelve years old.
3 I'm from Plymouth.

3 WORDS What's in the picture?

→ SB (p. 10)

a) ○ WB 05 Listen and write the numbers.

- 3 a big wheel
- 8 girls
- 1 the sea
- 7 a map
- 5 a hill
- 2 a boat
- 4 boys
- 6 a castle

b) Match the words to the numbers in a).

c) Finish with words from a).

I can see a b o a t on the s e a and an old c a s t l e on a h i l l. I can see two b o y s in a boat, two g i r l s and a m a p. And look! I can see a b i g w h e e l.

4 WORDS Silky's week

→ SB (p. 12)

TIP: Write days of the week with a CAPITAL letter.

a) ○ Write the days of the week in the right order.

ynduSa   usyaTed   yFaird   ynaMod   aWnseeddy   hysrauTd   tyaaSrud

1 Monday
2 Tuesday
3 Wednesday
4 Thursday
5 Friday
6 Saturday
7 Sunday

b) Read p. 12 in your student's book again and write the days in the puzzle. Then finish Silky's speech bubble.

1 Silky is at the Lido on …
2 She's in Plymouth Sound on …
3 Where is she on …? – She's at the Hoe.
4 She's at the Barbican on …
5 Where is she on …? – She's near the Aquarium.
6 And on …? – She's near the big wheel!

↓
1 W e d n e s d a y
2 T h u r s d a y
3 M o n d a y
4 T u e s d a y
5 S a t u r d a y
6 F r i d a y

The best day of the week is S u n d a y!

5 WORDS Animals ➜ SB (p. 15)

a) ○ Find and (circle) ten more animals in the word square. Label the pictures.

1 butterfly

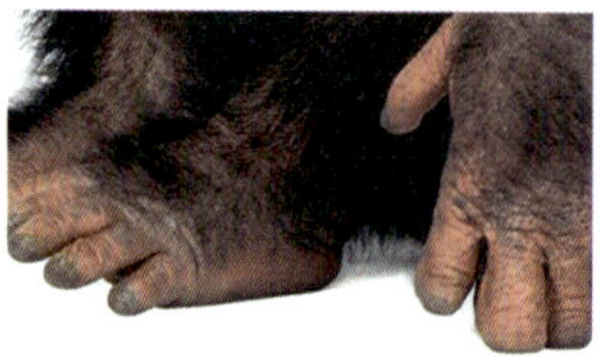

2 monkey

3 whale

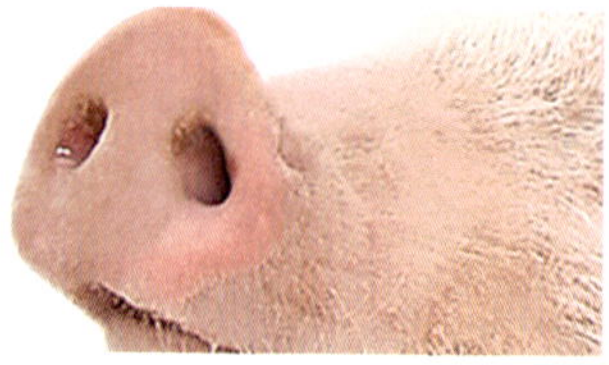

4 pig

5 dog

6 rat

7 snake

8 rabbit

b	u	t	t	e	r	f	l	y
g	i	m	o	n	k	e	y	r
b	e	a	r	s	n	a	k	e
e	l	e	p	h	a	n	t	a
r	a	t	f	w	h	a	l	e
r	a	b	b	i	t	d	o	g
f	p	i	g	e	a	n	t	☺

9 ant

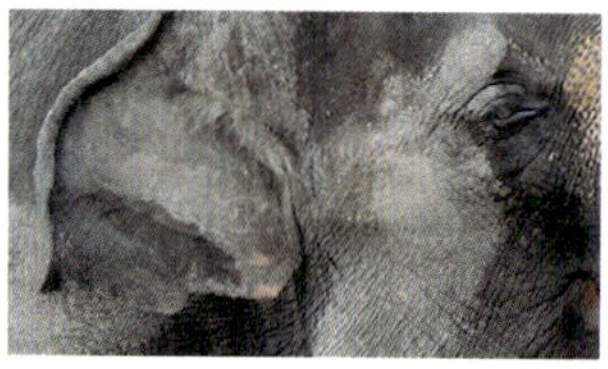

10 elephant

11 bear

b) ○ Finish Nina's speech bubble with the other letters in the word square in a). Draw and colour Nina's favourite animal.

My favourite animal is a

g i r a f f e.

c) What's your favourite animal? Write a sentence.

My favourite animal is a whale/horse ...

Nina's favourite animal

6 WORDS Colours ➜ *SB (p. 15)*

a) ○ Write the colours.

1 w h i t e 3 b r o w n 5 b l a c k 7 p i n k 9 y e l l o w

2 b l u e 4 r e d 6 g r e y 8 g r e e n 10 p u r p l e

b) What's the word in the blue boxes? Finish: Dan's favourite colour is o r a n g e.

c) What's your favourite colour? Write a sentence.

My favourite colour is yellow/red/blue/...

7 WORDS What's in the school bags? ➜ *SB (p. 16)*

a) ○ WB 06 Listen and write the numbers.

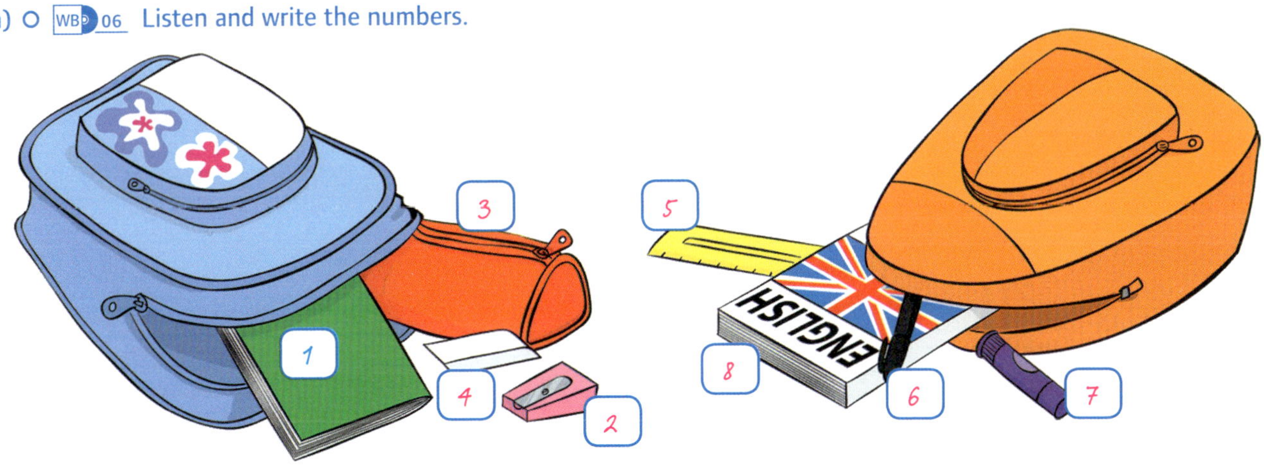

b) ● Write the name and the colour of the school things.

1 a green exercise book
2 a pink sharpener
3 a red pencil case
4 a white rubber
5 a yellow ruler
6 a black pen
7 a purple glue stick
8 a blue (and white) book

8 WORDS What's in the classroom? ➜ SB (p. 16)

a) Label the things in Dan's classroom. Use the box for help.

brdao · erostp · klcco · kdse · orod · wwdnio · cbrdaoup · rhica

1 window 2 clock 3 board

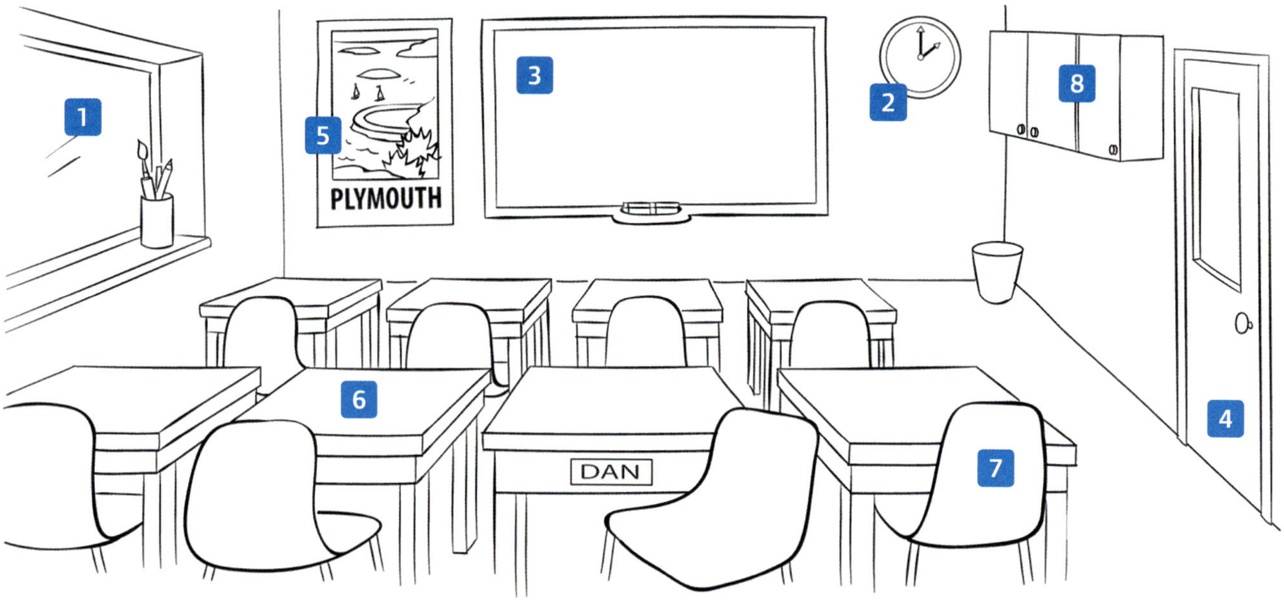

4 door 5 poster 6 desk 7 chair 8 cupboard

b) In the picture in a), draw and colour:

1 Dan's orange school bag on Dan's chair
2 a blue pencil case and a red exercise book on Dan's desk
3 a picture of Silky on the board

c) ● Write sentences about your classroom.

1 the door 2 the cupboard 3 the board 4 my desk

1 In my classroom the door is white/brown.
2 In my classroom the cupboard is (...).
3 In my classroom the board is (...).
4 In my classroom my desk is (...).

9 WORDS Numbers ➜ SB (p. 17)

a) Write the answers in the puzzle. Finish Dan's speech bubble with the word in the blue boxes.

1 one, … , five, seven
2 Silky is … years old.
3 two, four, six, …
4 fifteen, thirteen, …, nine
5 There are … days in a week.
6 five, ten, fifteen, …

			↓				
1			t	h	r	e	e
2		t	w	o			
3			e	i	g	h	t
4		e	l	e	v	e	n
5	s	e	v	e	n		
6	t	w	e	n	t	y	

I'm t w e l v e years old.

b) ○ Match.

34	forty	40
14	twenty-five	25
52	fourteen	18
43	eighty	13
30	fifty-two	80
	eighteen	
	forty-three	
	thirty-four	
	thirteen	
	thirty	

(Matched: 34 – thirty-four, 14 – fourteen, 52 – fifty-two, 43 – forty-three, 30 – thirty; forty – 40, twenty-five – 25, eighty – 80, eighteen – 18, thirteen – 13)

c) Write these numbers in words.

1 15 *fifteen*

2 19 *nineteen*

3 35 *thirty-five*

4 44 *forty-four*

5 78 *seventy-eight*

6 92 *ninety-two*

10 Telephone numbers ➔ *SB (p. 17)*

a) WB 07 Listen to Maria. Which is her phone number? A, B, C or D? (Circle) it.

A	B	C	D (circled)
07721 557038	07721 559138	07721 569038	07721 559038

b) ● WB 08 Listen and write the telephone numbers in Nina's book.

Dan	*228300*	Leo	*770662*
Charlotte	*240553*	Emily	*681338*
Noah	*991440*	Amira	*488075*

c) What's your telephone number (in words)? Write a sentence.

My telephone number is ...

d) Ask five friends their numbers and write them down. Then check.

11 The right time ➔ *SB (p. 17)*

a) WB 09 Listen and match the clocks. Write the letters (A–E) in the correct boxes.

b) Now write the times like this:

Clock A: *one forty-five*

Clock B: *two thirty*

Clock C: *two fifteen*

Clock D: *one thirty*

Clock E: *two fifty-five*

The first day at school

1 New students ➜ SB (pp. 20–21)

a) ○ Match and write the names.

Sam · Lucy · Bennett · Sen · Justin · Maya · Skinner · Pascoe

Maya Sen

Sam Bennett

Lucy Pascoe

Justin Skinner

b) Match and write two sentences each about Maya, Sam, Lucy and Justin.

She's at Plymstock School. · His mum and dad are in the navy. · His dad is in Boston. · Her school uniform is black. · He's late on the first day. · Her best friend is Maya. · She's at Coombe Dean. · He isn't from Plymouth.

1 About Maya: She's at Coombe Dean. Her school uniform is black.

2 About Sam: His mum and dad are in the navy. He isn't from Plymouth.

3 About Lucy: She's at Plymstock School. Her best friend is Maya.

4 About Justin: He's late on the first day. His dad is in Boston.

c) ● Finish the text with words from the box.

about · brother · dark · father · first · friends · from · late · navy · new · nice · school · students · their · time · where

It's the first day at school. Lucy, Sam and Justin are students at Plymstock. Their Plymstock uniform is nice. It's dark blue and grey. Maya is at Coombe Dean, but her brother is at Plymstock. Lucy and Maya are best friends. Sam is from London. He's new in Plymouth. His mother and father are in the navy. And what about Justin? Where is he? Oh, no! He's on Skype – and he's late. It's 8:15 in Plymouth, but what time is it in Boston?

2 What's right? (Personal pronouns) ➜ SB (p. 24)

Write the words and the right personal pronouns (he, she, it, they).

a card – it

Sam – he

pigs – they

a rubber – it

boys – they

trainers – they

a butterfly – it

Maya – she

a giraffe – it

a girl – she

3 Who says it (Personal pronouns) ➜ SB (p. 24)

Put in I, you, he, she, it, we or they. Who says it? Write the name.

Name:

Lucy: "My sister is at Plymstock. She 's in Year 9."

Maya: "Lucy, you 're my best friend, but I 'm at a different school. It 's sad."

Sam: "We 're new here. I like Plymouth. Mum and Dad too. They 're in the navy."

Justin: "I 'm on Skype with Dad. He 's in Boston. Oh, no! It 's 8:15."

4 New friends (*be*: positive and negative) ➜ SB (p. 25)

a) Finish with positive forms: 'm, 're, 's.

1 Lucy and Maya are best friends. They 're eleven.

2 Maya: Lucy is at Plymstock but I 'm at Coombe Dean.

3 Lucy: It 's sad. We're at different schools.

4 Sam is new in Plymouth. He 's from London.

5 Silky is from Plymouth. She 's a grey seal.

6 Silky: Come and meet my friends! They 're cool.

b) Finish with negative forms: 'm not, aren't, isn't.

1 Sam is from London. He isn't from Plymouth.

2 The students are eleven. They aren't twelve.

3 Lucy: We're at Plymstock. We aren't at Coombe Dean.

4 Sam: I 'm not from here. I'm from London.

5 Justin's dad is in Boston. He isn't in Plymouth.

6 Silky: I'm two. I 'm not three.

5 The student's pencils (The possessive) ➜ *SB (p. 26)*

a) ○ Match the letters A–F to the pictures 1–6.

1

3

5

2

4

6

A the student's pencils
B the students' pencils
C the boy's room
D the girls' rabbits
E the girl's rabbits
F the boys' room

b) ● Write the sentences again. Put the missing apostrophes ('s or s') in the underlined words.

1 What colour is Mayas uniform? *What colour is Maya's uniform?*

2 Where is the Sens flat? *Where is the Sens' flat?*

3 The boys names are Sam and Justin. *The boys' names are Sam and Justin.*

4 Lucy, is your sisters name Holly? *Lucy, is your sister's name Holly?*

6 Nina and Dan ➜ *SB (p. 26)*

a) WB 10 Listen to Nina and Dan. Are the sentences right or wrong? Circle a letter.

	Right	Wrong
1 Nina and Dan are from Plymouth.	(N)	M
2 Dan is in Year 8.	(I)	L
3 Nina is at Plymstock School.	A	(S)
4 Dan's sister is in Year 7.	U	(T)
5 Nina's classmates are nice.	(U)	C
6 Dan's favourite day is Saturday.	(J)	Y

b) In the right order, the correct letters spell the name of a Plymstock student. Who is it?

➜ The name of the student is *J u s t i n*.

7 About you ➜ *SB (p. 26)*

● WB 11 You are in Plymouth. You meet Nina. Listen and answer her questions.

TIP: For help, listen to exercise 6 again!

8 Dan's email

➜ SB (p. 26)

Read Dan's email. Then answer it. Write about yourself. You can change the green words. Write in your exercise book.

Hi!
My name is **Dan Miller**. I'm **twelve** years old and I'm from **Plymouth** in **England**.
I have a **sister, Gemma**. I have a cool **dog** too. I'm at **Plymstock School** in Year **8**.
I like my **classmates**, but I don't like **uniforms**.
My favourite colour is **orange** and my favourite animal is a **monkey**.
My favourite day is **Saturday**.
I **meet my friends** then.
What about you? Please write!
Bye! **Dan**

Hi Dan!

My name is ...

9 The teacher says ... (Imperatives)

➜ SB (p. 27)

a) ○ Finish the imperatives with a verb from the box, with or without don't.

be · forget · give · hurry up · *look* · put · *talk* · wear

1 *Look* at the board, please.

2 *Don't talk* to your friends in class.

3 *Give* me your exercise books, please.

4 *Put* your English book on your desk, please.

5 *Don't forget* your books.

6 *Hurry up*, please. You're late.

7 *Don't be* late for your lessons.

8 And *don't wear* trainers with your uniform.

b) ● Write two or three more sentences, with and without don't.

____

____

[1]Octavia [ɒk'teɪviə] [2]away [ə'weɪ] weg [3]Sidney ['sɪdni]

10 Yes, he is/No, he isn't (*be*: questions and short answers) ➜ *SB (p. 29)*

Read the text in your student's book on p. 28 again. Write short answers.

1 Is Justin late on the first day? – Yes, *he is* .

2 Is Miss Bell the new class teacher? – Yes, *she is* .

3 Is Sam in a football team? – No, *he isn't* .

4 Are Lucy's favourite animals guinea pigs? – No, *they aren't* .

5 Are Maya and Lucy at different schools? – Yes, *they are* .

6 Is Lucy from London? – No, *she isn't* .

7 Is your school big? – *Yes, it is. / No, it isn't.*

8 Are you at a new school now? – *Yes, I am. / No, I'm not.*

9 Are you and your best friend at different schools? – *Yes, we are. / No, we aren't.*

10 Is your favourite subject English? – *Yes, it is. / No, it isn't.*

11 Are your Mum and Dad from Boston? – *Yes, they are. / No, they aren't.*

11 WORDS School subjects ➜ *SB (p. 30)*

a) ○ Find five more school subjects. Colour the book pages and write the subjects.

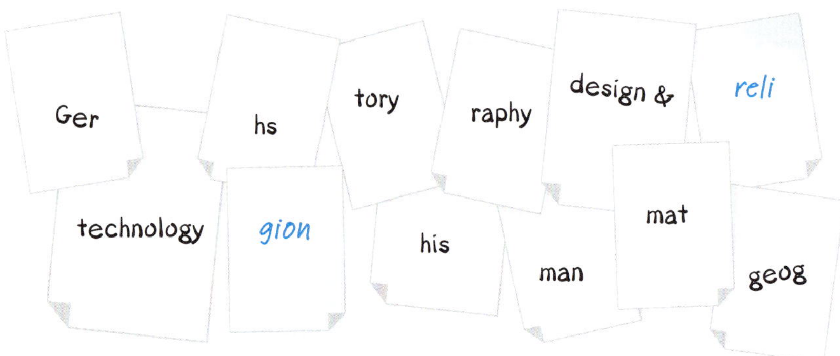

religion, geography, German,

design & technology, maths,

history

b) Now write the names of these subjects:

a r t

m u s i c

E n g l i s h

F r e n c h

P E

The letters in the blue boxes spell Dan's favourite subject. What is it? – It's *s c i e n c e* .

c) Finish the sentences.

1 My favourite subject is *(geography)* .

2 I like *(history)* and *(art)* too.

3 I don't like *(PE)* .

4 The first lesson on Monday is *(German)* .

5 We have three *(maths)* lessons every week.

[1]Sherman [ˈʃɜːrmən]

12 Is the timetable right? ➜ SB (p. 30)

● WB 12 Listen to Dan and his classmate Nick. Finish Nick's timetable. Listen two times.

Lesson	Monday	Tuesday	Wednesday	Thursday	Friday
9:00–10:00	French	History	English	Science	Maths
10:00–11:00	ICT	Science	German	French	Design & Technology
Break 11:00–11:20					
11:20–12:20	English	Design & Technology	Maths	History	English
12:20–1:20	Maths	Geography	Learning to learn	English	Music
Lunch 1:20–1:55					
1:55–2:55	Science	PE	Religion	Art	PE

13 An English student ➜ SB (p. 30)

An English student is at your school. Say hello to him.

Du sagst ihm, wie du heißt und fragst nach seinem Namen.

You: Hi! My name is ... What's your name?

Simon: Oh, hi! I'm Simon.

Du möchtest wissen, woher er kommt und wie seine Heimatstadt heißt.

You: Where are you from? What's the name of your hometown?

Simon: I'm from Plymouth. It's a big place, nice too.

Frage ihn, ob er Deutsch sprechen kann.

You: Can you speak German?

Simon: No, I can't, but I can say my name and my birthday.

Frag ihn nach seinem Lieblingsfach.

You: What's your favourite subject?

Simon: It's maths, but science is good too.

Du möchtest wissen, welche Farbe seine Schuluniform hat.

You: What colour is your school uniform?

Simon: It's dark blue. It's OK, but I don't like uniforms.

Du möchtest wissen, ob es deutsche Schüler und Schülerinnen an seiner Schule gibt.

You: Are there any German students at your school?

Simon: Two or three, but not in my class. OK. See you later. Bye!

14 SPELLING Apostrophes ➜ SB (p. 30)

● Put in the apostrophes (').

1 Wheres Maya? *Where's Maya?*

2 She isnt here. *She isn't here.*

3 Whos that? – Its Maya. *Who's that? – It's Maya.*

4 Thats Lucy! *That's Lucy!*

5 Dont be late! *Don't be late!*

6 We arent late. *We aren't late.*

7 Its two oclock. *It's two o'clock.*

8 Lets go! *Let's go!*

15 WORDS Months of the year ➜ SB (p. 31)

a) Find the code and write the names of eight months.

TIP: Write months of the year with a CAPITAL letter.

23 22 24 22 14 25 22 9
D e c e m b e r

14 26 2
M a y

12 24 7 12 25 22 9
O c t o b e r

14 26 9 24 19
M a r c h

17 6 15 2
J u l y

17 6 13 22
J u n e

17 26 13 6 26 9 2
J a n u a r y

21 22 25 9 6 26 9 2
F e b r u a r y

b) Four months are the same in German and English. Write the names. Can you say them in English?

April, August, September, November

16 WORDS Happy birthday! ➜ SB (p. 31)

a) WB 13 Listen and write the birthdays of Nina's friends in her book. Then finish the sentences.

Dan	*1st March*
Noah	*3rd May*
Emily	*5th June*
Leo	*12th July*
Charlotte	*30th October*
Amira	*22nd December*

1 Dan's birthday *is on the first of March.*

2 Noah's birthday *is on the third of May.*

3 Emily's birthday *is on the fifth of June.*

4 Leo's birthday *is on the twelfth of July.*

5 Charlotte's birthday *is on the thirtieth of October.*

6 Amira's birthday *is on the twenty-second of December.*

b) ● Write the birthdays of your mum, dad and best friend.

My mum's birthday ...

17 PRONUNCIATION *a* [ə] or *an* [ən] ➜ SB (p. 31)

WB 14 Say the words with a or an and write them in the correct list. Then listen to the CD and check.

yellow pen · exercise book · new word · hundred · hour · horse · answer · art lesson · uniform · ICT teacher · map · MP3 player

a [ə]	an [ən]
a yellow pen	an exercise book
a new word	an hour
a hundred	an answer
a horse	an art lesson
a uniform	an ICT teacher
a map	an MP3 player

18 REVISION WORDS Pairs[1] ➜ SB (p. 34)

a) Find and write pairs.

sister · there · with · Bye! · answer · without · brother · long · Hello! · here · right · old · catch · wrong · throw · ask · new · short

with – without	right – wrong	catch – throw
new – old	brother – sister	ask – answer
Hello! – Bye!	short – long	here – there

b) Finish the sentences with words from a).

1 Justin: Room HU9 isn't here. Where is it? Oh, look! It's there.

2 Miss Bell: Throw the ball and ask a question. Catch the ball and answer it.

3 Is Lucy's answer right or wrong?

4 Sam's trainers are new, but Justin's trainers are old.

5 Trainers with school uniform – no. Don't wear school uniform without black school shoes!

c) Write three more word pairs.

mum – dad, boy – girl, student – teacher, come – go

TIP: For help, look at the Vocabulary in your student's book, pp. 200–211.

[1] pair [peə] *Paar*

19 Plymstock School (*there is/there are*) ➔ SB (p. 34)

Finish the text with there is/there's, there are, there isn't, there aren't.

There's (1) a nice school in Plymstock – my school. There are (2) lots of classrooms in my school. There's (3) a computer room, but there aren't (4) any computer games. There isn't (5) a swimming pool, but there's (6) a big gym. There isn't (7) a restaurant[1], but there's (8) a nice canteen with red and yellow chairs. In my library there are (9) cupboards, chairs and desks – oh, and there are (10) books too! Animals? No, there aren't (11) any elephants or giraffes, but watch out! Sometimes there's (12) a strange monster in the library. Look! Can you see it? Haha! It's me! Morph!

20 Ask and answer (*there is/there are*: questions and short answers) ➔ SB (p. 34)

● You meet Sam in Plymouth. Write his questions with Is there a ...?/Are there any ...? Answer with short answers.

1 zoo[2]/town?
Sam: Is there a zoo in your town?
You: Yes, there is./No, there isn't.

2 any shops[3]/street?
Sam: Are there any shops in your street?
You: Yes, there are./No, there aren't.

3 canteen/school?
Sam: Is there a canteen in your school?
You: Yes, there is./No, there isn't.

4 any computers/classroom?
Sam: Are there any computers in your classroom?
You: Yes, there are./No, there aren't.

21 Silky can do it (*can/can't*) ➔ SB (p. 34)

a) Finish the sentences with can ☺ or can't ☹ and a verb from the box.

catch · find · see · sing · speak · spell

1 Silky can catch fish. ☺
2 Silky can see her friends every day. ☺
3 Maya can't speak German. ☹
4 Sam can't sing songs. ☹
5 Lucy can spell 'technology'. ☺
6 Justin can't find his pencil case. ☹

b) Write four questions with Can ...? for a partner. Ask about your partner's family/about the Plymouth kids/Silky ...

Can your brother do kung fu?

[1]restaurant ['restrɒnt] *Restaurant* [2]zoo [zuː] *Zoo* [3]shop [ʃɒp] *Laden*

22 SPELLING The alphabet ➜ SB (p. 35)

a) ○ WB 15 Listen, then say the alphabet.

b) WB 16 Now listen and colour the letters in a). You need a grey, green, red, blue and yellow pen.

c) Find and write the name of Dan's dog.

TIP: The colours under the letters can help you. Look at exercise 1a) again!

23 Pronunciation course ➜ SB (p. 35)

a) WB 17 Listen to words with the sounds [ʃ] (she), [tʃ] (chair) and [dʒ] (gym). Say each word at least twice.

Charlie · English · finish · geography · giraffe · June · March · match · orange · sharpener · shoe · show · strange · teacher · touch

b) ● Now put the words from a) in the right list:

[ʃ]	[tʃ]	[dʒ]
English	Charlie	geography
finish	March	giraffe
sharpener	match	June
shoe	teacher	orange
show	touch	strange

c) WB 18 Linking is important in English. We link vowel and consonant sounds to the next word. Listen and practise the sentences.

There‿are‿lots‿of‿animals‿in Plymouth. My favourite‿animal‿is‿a‿seal.

d) WB 19 Now say these sentences. Link words with ‿ as in c). You can record your voice. Then check.

1 What page are we on?
2 Can I open the window, please?
3 Can you say it again, please?

24 SPELLING Letters ➔ SB (p. 35)

a) ○ WB 20 Say it in English. Then listen and check.

1 CD 2 PC 3 DVD 4 TV

b) WB 21 Listen and write the family[1] names of Nina's friends.

1 Charlotte *Granger*

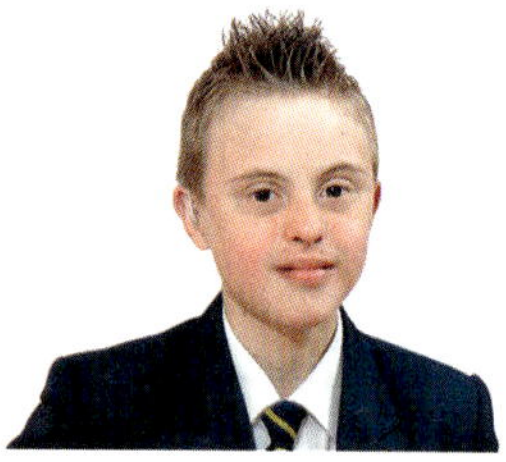

2 Leo *Cooper*

3 Emily *Harvey*

4 Amira *Patel*

5 Noah *Jenkins*

c) ● WB 22 Listen and write the pairs.

1 *eight* – *great*
2 *shoe* – *blue*
3 *wheel* – *seal*
4 *door* – *four/for*
5 *chair* – *bear*
6 *bird* – *word*

25 MIXED BAG After school *(be, there is/are, imperatives, yes, it is/No, it isn't, can/can't)* ➔ SB (p. 37)

● Put in the missing word or words.

Mum: Lucy, *are* you back?

Lucy: Yes, *I am*.

Mum: Hi! How*'s* the new school and *who*'s your teacher?

Lucy: I'm in 7EB and my teacher *is* Miss Bell. *She's* nice. And the school is cool.

Mum: And *are* your classmates OK? *Are there* any nice girls?

Lucy: Yes, *there are*. Boys too. There's Sam. He *isn't* from Plymouth. He's from London.
And *there's* Justin. Plymstock is great. *It's* so big.
There are lots of computers and a big library.

Mum: And *what's* for homework? *Don't* forget your homework on the first day!

Lucy: But *where* are my new books? They *aren't* in my school bag.
Oh, no! *They're* on my desk in school! So I *can't* do my homework.

[1] family ['fæməli] *Familien-*

26 TEXT Chaos at the corner shop ➜ SB (pp. 36–37)

a) ○ Look at pp. 36–37 of your student's book again. Write the names.

1 Maya is late.
2 Sam can do kung fu.
3 Lily is Sam's little sister.
4 Maya is a good swimmer.
5 Lucy is Maya's best friend.
6 Sam is always with a group of boys.

b) Who says what? Match the pictures and the sentences.

Maya

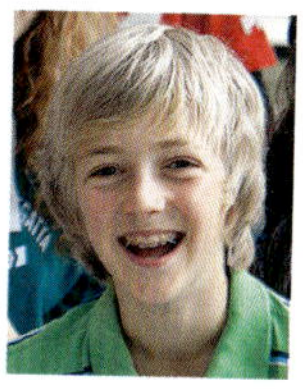
Sam

- A Maya is the best swimmer in Plymstock!
- B I know you from the Lido.
- C Sam, this is my best friend Maya.
- D Girls can't swim like boys.
- E My sister? Oh no! Where's Lily?
- F Our class teacher is …
- G You're always in that big group of boys.
- H Sorry, Dad … I'm late.
- I Go and find the yoghurt, little sister.

Lucy

c) Put the sentences in b) in the right order.

1 H
2 F
3 I
4 C
5 B
6 G
7 D
8 A
9 E

d) Now Sam is at home with his dad. Finish the dialogue with sentences from the box.

Dad: How's your new school? Is it nice?
Sam: Yes, it is. It's big too.
Dad: And what about your teacher?
Sam: Her name is Miss Bell. She's friendly.
Dad: And your new classmates? Are they nice?
Sam: There's a nice boy, Justin. And a girl, Lucy.
Dad: Are they your new friends?
Sam: Yes, they are. That's right.
Dad: Great! Now, how's your timetable?
Sam: The first break is at 11 o'clock and the lunch break is at 1:20.
Dad: And what about your lessons …?

> Great! Now, how's your timetable? ·
> Yes, it is. It's big too. ·
> The first break is at 11 o'clock and the lunch break is at 1:20. ·
> Are they your new friends? ·
> Her name is Miss Bell. She's friendly.

e) ● Write a short dialogue for Justin and his mum in your exercise book. You can use words/sentences from d).

1 WORDS Don't be late

Finish the sentences.

1 Mum: Don't be *l a t e* on your first day at school!

2 Miss Bell: Can you *s p e l l* 'cupboard', please?

3 Lucy: When's French? – Sam: Look at your *t i m e t a b l e*.

4 Justin: I don't like school shoes. I like my old *t r a i n e r s*!

5 Sam: Hurry up, Justin. We can't *w a i t* for you.

6 Lucy and Maya: We're best *f r i e n d s*.

7 Sam: My *b i r t h d a y* is in September.

8 Lucy: The chairs in the *c a n t e e n* are red and yellow.

9 Maya: Let's *m e e t* in the Broadway at 4:30.

10 Miss Bell: Don't write in your student's book. Write in your *e x e r c i s e b o o k*, please.

2 It's big (Personal pronouns)

Finish the sentences with the right personal pronoun (he, she, it, …).

1 Plymstock is our new school. *It* 's big.

2 Lucy is at Plymstock. *She* 's in Year 7.

3 Lucy and Sam like their new classmates. *They* 're nice.

4 Mukesh is Maya's brother. *He* 's in Year 9.

5 The students like their new timetable. *It* 's OK.

6 They like their new English books too. *They* 're cool.

3 An email (*be*: mixed forms)

Finish Justin's email to his dad with forms of be ('s/is/isn't, 're/are/…).

Hi, Dad!

This *is* (1) a photo of my new school. It *'s/is* (2) cool, big too – there *are* (3) 1,600 students! My classmates *are* (4) OK, and I like our class teacher. She *'s/is* (5) nice. Sam *is* (6) a new friend. He *isn't* (7) from Plymouth. He *'s/is* (8) from London. There *'s/is* (9) a nice girl too, Lucy. I *'m/am* (10) at home now. My friends *aren't* (11) here. They *'re/are* (12) in the Broadway. Your email says: *Are* (13) you happy at your new school? The answer *is* (14): Yes, I *am* (15)!

Bye!

Justin

4 Where are they?

WB 23 Where are Nick and Dan? Listen and tick (✓) a box. A, B, C or D?

1 A ☐ at home C ☐ in a shop
B ☐ in the gym D ☑ in the classroom

2 A ☐ at home C ☑ in a shop
B ☐ in the gym D ☐ in the classroom

5 A party

WB 24 First read the sentences. Then listen to the students. Are the sentences right or wrong? Tick (✓) a box.

	Right	Wrong
1 Charlotte is Nina's best friend.	✓	
2 It's Charlotte's thirteenth birthday on Saturday.		✓
3 Nina's friends can go to the party too.	✓	
4 Charlotte's telephone number is 240533.		✓
5 Charlotte's house[1] number is 40.	✓	
6 The name of the street is R E S C H L E I G H Avenue.		✓
7 The party is on 13th October.		✓
8 Dan's football training is on the day of the party.	✓	
9 There's a bus[2] to Charlotte's house at three thirty-five.	✓	
10 Dan can wear his football boots[3] at the party.		✓

Check: Listening

a) Vergleiche deine Antworten mit den Lösungen auf Seite 84 im Workbook.
b) Schätze deine Antworten mit einem grünen oder roten Gesicht ein.

4 Where are they?
Hast du beide Male verstanden, wo sich Dan und Nick befinden? ○ ○ → 5

5 A party
1 Hast du die Telefonnummer richtig verstanden? ○ ○ → 3
2 Hast du die Schreibweise des Straßennamens richtig verstanden (z. B. die Buchstaben *A, E, I, G, R*)? ○ ○ → 1
3 Hast du die Zahlen richtig verstanden (z. B. *thirteen, thirty, thirty-five*)? ○ ○ → 2
4 Hast du die Uhrzeiten problemlos verstanden? ○ ○ → 4
5 Hast du den Hörtext insgesamt gut verstanden? ○ ○ → 6

c) Wenn du dich rot eingeschätzt hast, schau dir die rechte Spalte an.
Die Nummern führen dich zu den passgenauen Übungen im Skills Training (S. 22–23).
Dort kannst du gezielt Hörverstehen trainieren.

[1] house [haʊs] *Haus, Haus-* [2] bus [bʌs] *Bus* [3] football boots [buːts] *Fußballschuhe*

1 The alphabet

a) WB 25 Listen and write the letter.

> **TIP:** For help, listen to the alphabet again (p. 17, exercise 22 in your workbook).

1 E 4 A 7 J 10 V

2 H 5 R 8 Y 11 Q

3 I 6 G 9 W 12 K

b) WB 26 Circle the letter you hear.

1 **A** / E 3 J / **G** 5 **I** / Y 7 **V** / W

2 A / **R** 4 **K** / Q 6 **E** / I 8 **J** / G

c) WB 27 Circle the letters you hear.

1 **OO** / W 2 **EA** / IE 3 EI / **AI** 4 UI / **UY** 5 **EE** / II

2 Numbers

a) WB 28 Circle the number you hear.

1 **30** / 13 3 70 / **17** 5 **18** / 80 7 **19** / 90 9 68 / **86** 11 93 / **39**

2 **15** / 50 4 **60** / 16 6 **14** / 40 8 34 / **43** 10 45 / **54** 12 **87** / 78

b) WB 29 Listen and write the number you hear.

1 32 3 23 5 84 7 65

2 48 4 56 6 79 8 97

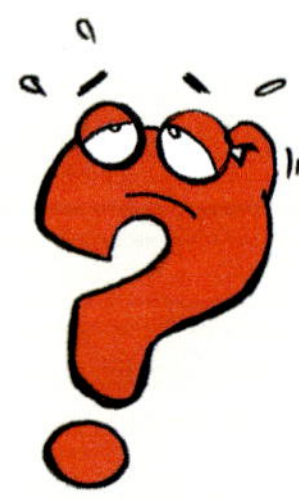

3 Telephone numbers

WB 30 Listen. What are the correct telephone numbers? Tick (✓) a box.

1 Nina's number:

A ☐ 01752 – 006 799
B ☐ 01725 – 660 799
C ✓ 01752 – 660 799
D ☐ 01752 – 600 799

2 Her dad's mobile number:

A ☐ 07700 – 994 511
B ☐ 07707 – 994 155
C ☐ 07007 – 449 115
D ✓ 07700 – 944 155

3 Her mum's mobile number:

A ☐ 07103 – 228 867
B ☐ 07700 – 288 276
C ✓ 07700 – 822 776
D ☐ 07713 – 822 788

4 What time is it?

WB 31 Listen and tick (✓) the time you hear.

1

A ☐ B ☑

3

A ☐ B ☑

5

A ☑ B ☐

7

A ☑ B ☐

2

A ☐ B ☑

4

A ☑ B ☐

6

A ☐ B ☑

8

A ☐ B ☑

5 Hello!

a) WB 32 Listen to Nina and Dan. Tick (✓) the correct box. The students talk about …

TIP: Konzentriere dich auf das Thema.

A ☐ their school.
B ☐ their teachers.
C ☐ their friends.
D ☑ their homes.

b) WB 33 Listen to Nina, Dan and Nick. Tick (✓) the correct box. They talk about …

A ☐ their favourite sport.
B ☐ their favourite people.
C ☑ their favourite animals.
D ☐ their favourite things.

6 It's Saturday

a) WB 34 Listen to Nina, Dan, Nick and Amira. Tick (✓) a box.

They talk about …

A ☐ the history of Plymouth. **B** ☑ places to go in Plymouth. **C** ☐ sport in Plymouth.

b) WB 34 Read the sentences and listen again. Are the sentences right or wrong? Tick (✓) a box.

TIP:
1. Hören: Beantworte die Aufgaben, die du schon kannst.
2. Hören: Konzentriere dich auf die Aufgaben, die du noch nicht beantwortet hast.

	Right	Wrong
1 It's Saturday at 8:30.	☐	☑
2 Nina is for the Aquarium.	☑	☐
3 There are 24 capsules[1] on the big wheel.	☐	☑
4 The big wheel is not Amira's favourite thing in Plymouth.	☑	☐
5 Amira is a good swimmer.	☐	☑
6 There aren't any tours of the Citadel on Saturdays.	☑	☐
7 The tours start at 2:30 on Tuesdays and Fridays.	☐	☑
8 The Barbican is Amira's favourite place.	☑	☐
9 From the Barbican you can see seals on the rocks[2].	☑	☐
10 The students talk about Plymouth Hoe.	☐	☑

[1]capsule ['kæpsjuːl] *Gondel* [2]rock [rɒk] *Felsen*

Homes and families

1 WORDS Our house ➜ SB (pp. 44–45)

Label the rooms and places in Dan's house.

bathroom · bedroom (2 x) · dining room · downstairs · garden · kitchen · living room · upstairs

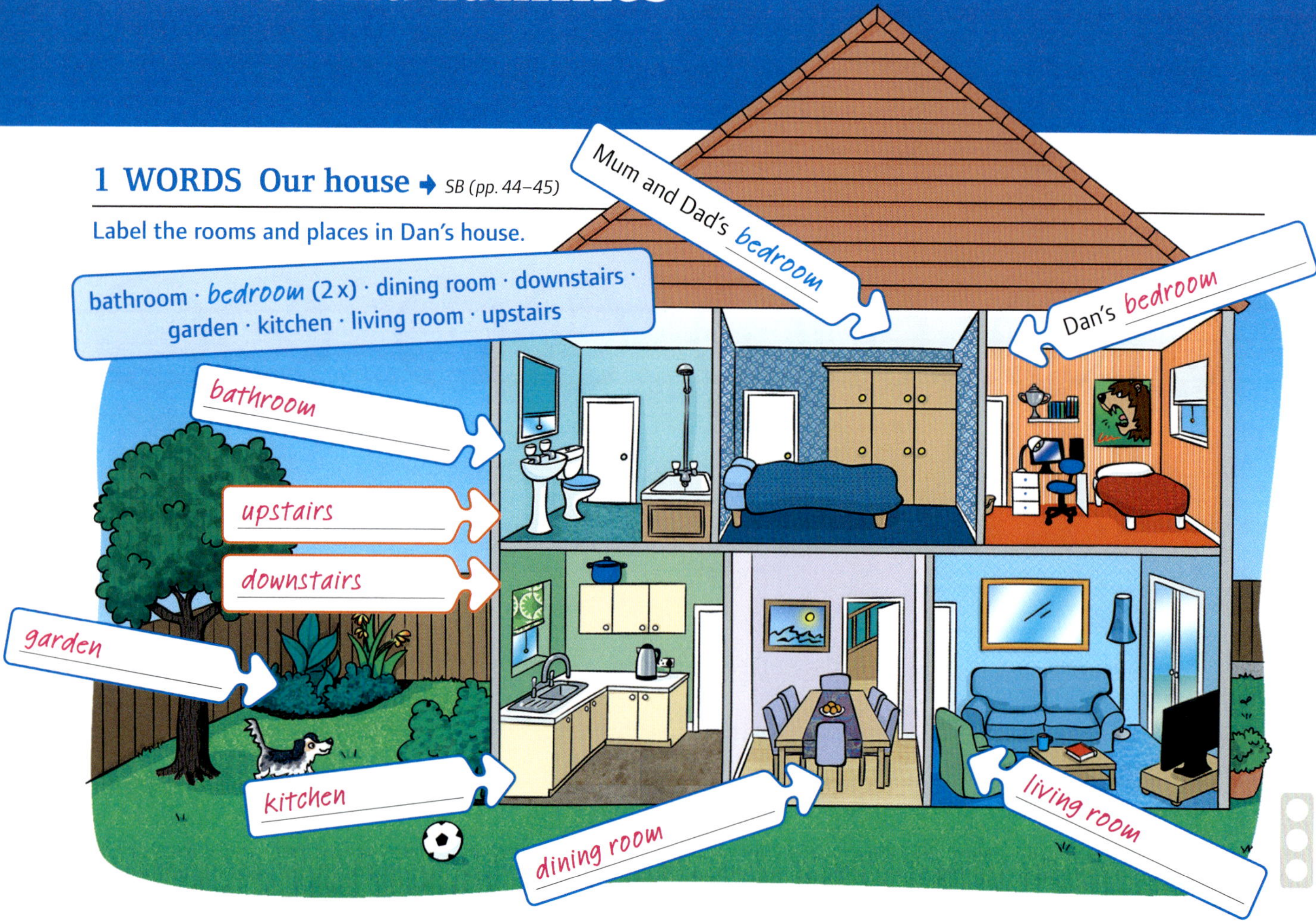

2 WORDS At home ➜ SB (pp. 44–45)

a) ○ Circle the names of ten more things in Dan's house.

s	o	f	a	T	d	e	s	k
c	m	y	f	V	t	a	p	v
u	l	a	m	p	o	o	i	u
p	c	r	c	i	i	t	c	e
b	l	s	h	e	l	f	t	a
o	o	r	a	b	e	d	u	m
a	c	c	i	h	t	a	r	i
r	k	r	r	i	s	g	e	r
d	e	t	a	b	l	e	e	n

→
- sofa
- desk
- lamp
- shelf
- bed
- table

↓
- TV
- cupboard
- clock
- chair
- toilet
- picture

b) In Dan's speech bubble, write a sentence with the extra letters in the word square[1]. Dan says:

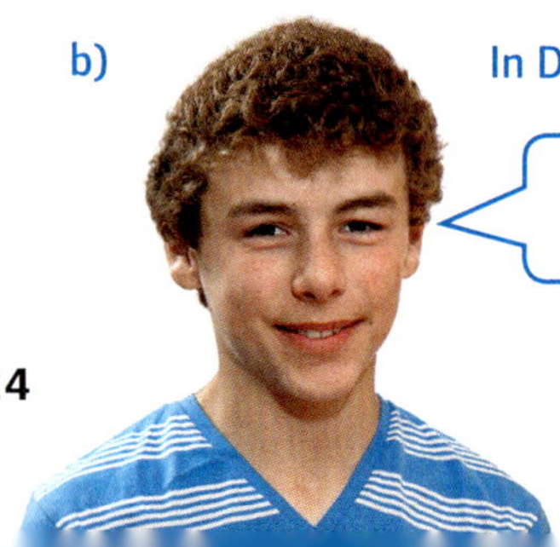

My favourite armchair is green!

[1] square [skweə] *Quadrat*

3 Dan's room ➔ SB (p. 47)

TIP:
dt.: Dans Zimmer
engl.: Dan's room

a) ● Look at the picture and read the text. There are six more wrong things. Find and (circle) the wrong things in the text.

Dan's favourite place is his bedroom. It's upstairs, near the bathroom and his mum and dad's room. From the window you can see the garden and the road. His bedroom is (grey) and orange. Orange is his favourite colour. The room isn't big, but it's nice. His bed is near the window in the corner. There's a cool picture of a (horse) in the corner too. Charlie's basket is on the floor near the (window). Then there's Dan's desk and a blue (armchair). Oh, and his dad's old computer is on the desk too. He can do his homework there. There are two shelves. The big shelf is for his books and school things. The small shelf is for CDs and games. Oh, and there's a lamp on the (floor). There's a nice photo of Charlie on the (small) shelf too. There are two posters on his cupboard – an (animal) poster and a poster of his favourite rock band. His favourite things are in his cupboard: his football and sports things, his skateboard and his old toys – oh, and his school uniform – but that isn't a favourite thing.

b) ● Now, correct the wrong sentences from the text.

1 *His bedroom is white and orange.*

2 *There's a cool picture of a lion in the corner too.*

3 *Charlie's basket is on the floor near the door.*

4 *Then there's Dan's desk and a blue chair.*

5 *Oh, and there's a lamp on the desk.*

6 *There's a nice photo of Charlie on the big shelf too.*

7 *There are two posters on his cupboard – a football poster and a poster of his favourite rock band.*

4 My bedroom ➔ SB (p. 47)

TIP: Exercises 2 and 3 can help you.

a) WB 35 Listen to Dan and Nina. They talk about their rooms. What are their questions?

b) ● WB 36 Now, answer Nina's questions about your bedroom. Press the pause button.[1]

Nina: Tell me about your room. Is it big?
You: …

Nina: What colour is it?
You: …

[1] Press the pause button. [pres ðə 'pɔːz ˌbʌtn] *Drück die Pausetaste.*

5 Silly Dan! ➔ *SB (p. 47)*

a) ○ Read Dan's speech bubble. The green words are in the wrong place.

I **have two lessons** at quarter past seven every morning. First I **text** Charlie in the kitchen. Then I **have lunch** with Mum and Gemma. Gemma and I **go home** at eight-thirty. At school we **wake up** before the break. At 1:20 we **play football** in the canteen. We **go to school** at three o'clock in the afternoon. After school I **watch TV** on the Hoe with my friends. In the evening I **have breakfast** in the living room, and before bed I **feed** my friends.

b) Write the text again with the green words in the right place. When you use a green word or phrase, ~~cross~~ it from the text in a).

*I **wake up** at quarter past seven every morning. First I **feed** Charlie in the kitchen. Then I **have breakfast** with Mum and Gemma. Gemma and I **go to school** at eight-thirty. At school we **have two lessons** before the break. At 1:20 we **have lunch** in the school canteen. We **go home** at three o'clock in the afternoon. After school I **play football** on the Hoe with my friends. In the evening I **watch TV** in the living room, and before bed I **text** my friends.*

6 PRONUNCIATION The "s"-sound ➔ *SB (p. 49)*

a) ● WB 37 Listen. What can you hear at the end of the word? Tick (✓) the right box.

	[s]	[z]	[ɪz]
1	✓		
2		✓	
3			✓
4		✓	
5	✓		
6		✓	
7			✓
8			✓
9	✓		
10	✓		

b) Say the words. Colour the "s"-sounds red [s], green [z] or blue [ɪz]:

1 acts
2 answers
3 catches
4 knows
5 counts
6 swims
7 touches
8 waits
9 watches
10 thinks

c) ● Can you say Sherman's tongue twister[1] three times?

[1] tongue twister ['tʌŋ twɪstə] *Zungenbrecher*

7 Abby's day (Simple present: positive sentences) ➜ *SB (p. 49)*

Look at the pictures and finish the sentences about Abby's day.

1

wake up – 7:00

3

have breakfast – family

5

eat – canteen

7

watch TV – family

2

feed Skip

4

start – 8:45

6

go for a walk – Skip

8

text – friends

1 In the week *Abby wakes up at 7:00.*

2 First *she feeds Skip.*

3 Then *she has breakfast with the family.*

4 School *starts at 8:45.*

5 At 1:20 *she eats in the canteen.*

6 After school *she goes for a walk with Skip.*

7 In the evening *she watches TV with the family.*

8 Before bed *she texts her friends.*

8 Charlie (Simple present: positive sentences) ➜ *SB (p. 49)*

Finish Dan's text about his dog.

I *feed* (feed) Charlie before school. He *eats* (eat) a lot, and there's always a swimming pool in the kitchen. Then he *plays* (play) in the garden and *watches* (watch) the birds. Before lunch he *goes* (go) to the shops with Mum. After school we *play* (play) football with him in the garden. In the evening Mum and Dad *go* (go) for a walk with him. They *throw* (throw) his ball and he *catches* (catch) it – but not always. He *runs* (run) away with the ball and Mum and Dad can't find it. That's Charlie's favourite game. He *has* (have) a new ball every week. In the evening we *play* (play) games. Charlie *falls* (fall) asleep in his basket – or on my bed!

9 Abby and her family ➜ *SB (p. 49)*

● Write six or more sentences about Abby and her family in your exercise book.

TIP: For help, read pp. 47–48 in your student's book again.

Abby lives in Wembury with her family. They have a house in Beach Road.
Abby likes ...

10 The right order, please! (Word order) ➜ *SB (p. 49)*

Write correct sentences.

1 like · their new teacher · the kids — *The kids like their new teacher.*

2 they · every day · have · five lessons — *They have five lessons every day.*

3 in the park · plays · on Saturdays · football · Sam — *Sam plays football in the park on Saturdays.*

4 helps · after school · Maya · at home · her mum — *Maya helps her mum at home after school.*

5 in his room · his homework · Sam · does · after school — *Sam does his homework in this room after school.*

6 to the sailing club · goes · Abby · on Sundays — *Abby goes to the sailing club on Sundays.*

7 in the afternoon · to the beach · Tim and Skip · go — *Tim and Skip go to the beach in the afternoon.*

8 crabs · in a pool · catches · Silky · in the evening — *Silky catches crabs in a pool in the evening.*

11 STUDY SKILLS Words in groups ➜ *SB (p. 50)*

a) ○ One word in each[1] group is different. Cross it out (x).
Then find an umbrella word for the group.

1 twelve fifteen forty eleven ~~week~~ — 1 *numbers*

2 Tuesday Sunday Friday ~~January~~ Thursday — 2 *days of the week*

3 pencil case glue stick ~~crab~~ ruler book — 3 *school bag*

4 lessons classroom uniform ~~bedroom~~ teacher — 4 *school*

5 armchair ~~shop~~ living room sofa bed — 5 *home/house*

6 canteen gym ~~student~~ library corner shop — 6 *places*

b) Make a mind map about 'weekdays'. Use the words in the box and add more words.
Write in your exercise book.

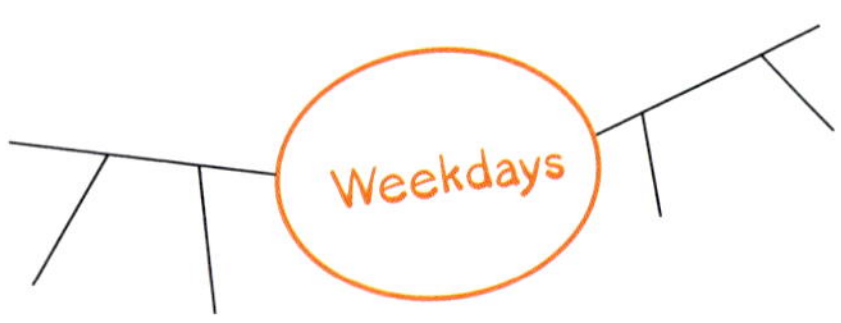

in the morning · read · meet friends · text friends · in the afternoon · have dinner · in the evening · watch TV · have lessons · help at home · have breakfast · write emails · make my bed · do my homework · play football/computer games

12 On weekdays ➜ *SB (p. 50)*

Choose your favourite weekday and tell the class about what you do then.
Say six or more sentences.

TIP: For more ideas look at exercise 7, p. 27 again. Use your mind map from exercise 11b).

go in the bathroom · have breakfast · go to school · go home · do my homework · text/meet my friends · watch TV

1 My favourite weekday is … On … I wake up at …

2 Then I …

3 After that I …

4 School starts at … We have … lessons.

5 After school I …

6 In the afternoon/evening I … We eat at …

[1] each [iːtʃ] *jede/r/s*

13 Pronunciation course ([θ] and [ð]) ➜ SB (p. 51)

a) WB 38 Words with the sound [θ]. Listen and practise:

thanks · third · three · tenth · month · birthday

b) WB 39 Words with the sound [ð]. Listen and practise:

there · that · then · this · mother · without · with

c) ● WB 40 Now listen and match the words to the correct sound:

sound [θ]	sound [ð]
think	brother
Thursday	them
fourth	they
throw	father

d) WB 41 Say these words with the correct word stress. You can record your voice. Then listen and check.

classmate · geography · telephone · umbrella · orange · uniform · subject · family · religion · surprised · trophy · July · history

14 Nina Hunt's family (Simple present: negative sentences) ➜ SB (p. 54)

○ Finish the sentences about Nina with don't or doesn't.

1 Nina and her family don't live in Wembury.
2 Nina doesn't go to Plymstock.
3 Nina's sister doesn't like sport.
4 The Hunts don't have a dog.
5 Nina's sister doesn't like dogs.
6 Nina's mum and dad don't have time for animals.

15 The Sens (Simple present: negative sentences) ➜ (p. 54)

Are the sentences right or wrong? Correct the wrong sentences with don't or doesn't.

TIP: You can find the answers on p. 52 of your student's book.

1 The Sens live in a house. Wrong. The Sens don't live in a house.
2 Mukesh goes to Plymstock. Right.
3 Mukesh likes cricket. Wrong. Mukesh doesn't like cricket.
4 Maya goes sailing. Right.
5 Mukesh has time for sport. Wrong. Mukesh doesn't have time for sport.
6 Maya and Mukesh know about their family. Wrong. Maya and Mukesh don't know about their family.
7 The Sens all live in India and Britain. Wrong. The Sens don't all live in India and Britain.
8 Cousin Dilip lives in London. Wrong. Cousin Dilip doesn't live in London.

16 Morph doesn't do homework (Simple present: positive and negative sentences) ➜ SB (p. 54)

Finish the sentences with a positive or negative form of the verb in brackets ( ).

1 Morph *doesn't do* (~~do~~) homework.

2 Sam *does* (do) kung fu.

3 Morph *doesn't play* (~~play~~) cricket.

4 Sam *doesn't go* (~~go~~) sailing.

5 The Bennetts *don't live* (~~live~~) in Wembury.

6 Lucy and Holly *don't go* (~~go~~) to Coombe Dean.

7 Lucy's grandma and grandpa *live* (live) on a farm.

8 Lucy often *feeds* (feed) the animals with Grandpa.

9 Holly *doesn't feed* (~~feed~~) the animals.

10 At the weekend Holly *sleeps* (sleep) till lunch.

17 An email ➜ SB (p. 54)

● Write an email to Lucy. Tell her what you and your best friend do and don't do at the weekend. Write eight or more sentences. You can use the words in the boxes. Write in your exercise book.

My name is … · I live in … · My best friend's name is … · He/She doesn't live/lives near here · he/she often comes to our flat at the weekend · We often … or we …

play football/tennis/computer games · watch DVDs · text/meet friends · go to the shops/the park · do our homework

Hi Lucy!

____

18 WORDS Nina's family tree ➜ SB (p. 55)

● WB 42 Look at Nina's family tree. Then listen and (circle) the right name.

1 Carla, (Louise), Maria

2 Pippa, Carla, (Maria)

3 Ben, (William), Steve

4 Maria, Nina, (Carla)

5 William, Ben, (Luke)

6 (Nina), Carla, Louise

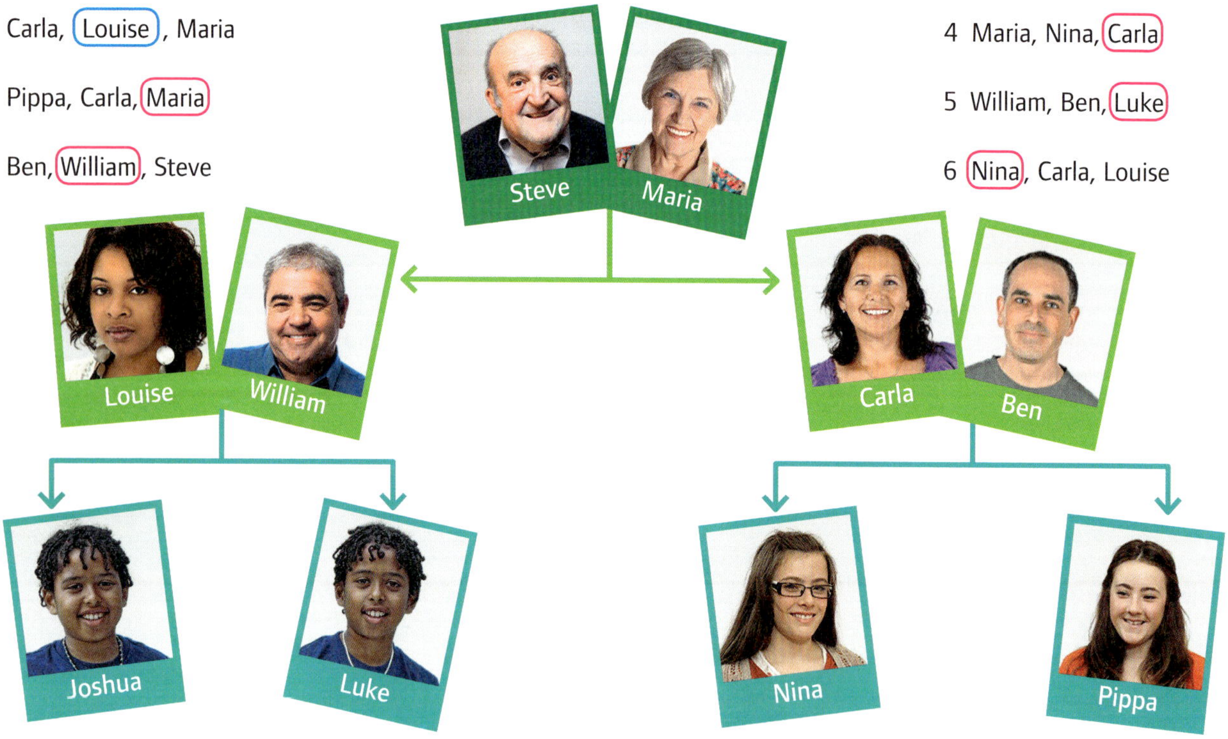

19 WORDS Nina's family ➜ SB (p. 55)

○ Look at the family tree in exercise 18 again and finish what Nina says about her family.

Nina

"My family? OK. Here we go! My *mum/mother*'s name is Carla, and my *dad/father*'s name is Ben. They're OK. Pippa is my big *sister*. She's thirteen. She thinks she's cool, but she likes computer games with silly monsters. Steve is our *grandfather/grandpa*. He's great. He often forgets things – like our names, but he knows all about sport. He plays cricket and golf. *Grandmother/Grandma*'s name is Maria. She's cool. She likes kung fu and computer games. Our *aunt*'s name is Louise. She's nice. She has six cats and three birds. Our *uncle*'s name is William. He's my mum's *brother*. Joshua and Luke are his kids – our *cousins*. They're twins. Pippa thinks they're mad, but I think they're cool. They often do silly things – so? What about your family? Are they all mad too?"

20 About your family ➜ SB (p. 55)

● Look at your family tree. Then tell a partner about three people in your family. Say two or more sentences about each person. Exercise 19 can help you.

I have a little brother. He's cool. He always throws his toys on the floor.
My uncle ... is my mum's /dad's brother. He plays football with us in the park.

21 WORDS Food puzzle ➜ SB (p. 57)

a) Write the names of the food in the puzzle. What's the word in the blue boxes?

6

1

2

9

				↓						
1			c	r	e	a	m			
2			y	o	g	h	u	r	t	
3			j	a	m					
4				s	o	u	p			
5		p	o	t	a	t	o	e	s	
6				b	r	e	a	d		
7		c	h	e	e	s	e			
8	v	e	g	e	t	a	b	l	e	s
9				f	r	u	i	t		

8

7

5

3

4

b) Write the word in the blue boxes.

→ Sam's favourite food is *roast beef*.

[1] my mother

22 What would you like to eat? ➜ SB (p. 58)

● Together with your German cousin and your aunt you are at Plymouth harbour. They don't speak much English. Help them to get something to eat and drink.

You: Schau, da ist ein Imbissstand. Wollen wir schauen, was sie haben?

Aunt: Für mich würde ein belegtes Brot und etwas zu trinken reichen. Hab keinen großen Hunger.

You: We'd like sandwiches and something to drink, please.

Man: Well, I have lots of sandwiches: cheese, chicken, salami, crab, roast beef … all fresh.

You (to aunt): Er hat verschiedene Brote, … mit Käse, Salami, Krabbenfleisch, Rinderbraten, …

Aunt: Dann nehme ich zwei Stück, eins mit Käse und eins mit Rinderbraten.

Cousin: Ich möchte keine Brote.

You (to man): Two sandwiches, please. One with cheese and one with roast beef.

Man: And what would you like to drink? There are hot and cold drinks: tea, coffee, water, cola, …

You (to aunt): Er fragt, was ihr trinken wollt: Tee, Kaffee, Wasser, Cola …

Aunt: Ich möchte eine Tasse Tee – englisch natürlich.

Cousin: Und ich möchte eine große Cola.

You (to man): A cup of tea and a big cola, please.

Man: Would you like dessert? There's fruit salad, cheese cake, scones with jam or ice cream.

You (to aunt): Er hat auch Obstsalat, Käsekuchen, Scones und Eis.

Cousin: Was sind denn *scones*? Naja, ich möchte lieber ein großes Schokoladeneis, ohne Sahne bitte.

You (to man): And a big chocolate ice cream, please.

Aunt: Frag ihn, wieviel es kostet. Hier ist Geld. Hoffentlich ist das genug.

You (to man): How much is that, please?

23 My new friend (*my, your, his …*) ➜ SB (p. 58)

Put in *my*, *your*, *his* …

Maya: I have a new friend. Her name is Abby Blackwell. The Blackwells live in Wembury.

Their house is near the beach. It's very nice.

Mukesh: Is Abby in your class?

Maya: No, she's at Plymstock. She has two brothers. Their names are Tim and Will.

She has a dog too. His name is Skip, and there's a cat,

but I can't remember its name.

Mukesh: Oh, so she's a nice girl. You can invite Abby to our flat. Ask Mum. But what about Lucy?

Maya: Abby is nice, but Lucy is my best friend.

24 What's correct? (there, they're, their) ➔ SB (p. 58)

● Finish the dialogue with: there, their, they're.

Dan: Where are my football shoes?

Nick: Your football shoes? Well, they're usually over there in the corner.

Dan: But they're not there now.

Nick: Maybe they're in a different place today. In the other corner?

Dan: No. Ali and Samir always put their shoes in that corner.

Nick: But Ali and Samir are wearing their sports things now.

Dan: Right. But look, there are some shoes under that chair. Maybe …

Nick: But they can't be *your* shoes. They're clean!

25 TEXT Saturday in Plymouth ➔ SB (pp. 60–61)

a) Read the story on pp. 60–61 of your student's book again. (Circle) the correct letter. You need[1] the letters in part b).

1 Justin goes to the harbour with …
- B Tom.
- (N) his mum.
- P a friend from school.

2 At the harbour Justin …
- R has an ice cream.
- M takes a boat tour.
- (S) films the boats.

3 Justin starts to film at …
- L 3:45.
- (B) 3:46.
- Y 4:45.

4 The next harbour boat tour is at …
- (T) four o'clock.
- O quarter past four.
- U half past four.

5 At the harbour Justin's favourite boat is …
- A the Blue Bird.
- T a navy ship.
- (O) a big sailing boat.

6 Tom, the little boy, has …
- Y a white T-shirt, jeans, red trainers.
- S a red T-shirt, jeans, blue trainers.
- (O) a red T-shirt, jeans, white trainers.

b) In the right order, the correct letters from a) give you a place name. → It is B O S T O N.

c) ● Write the missing words. In the correct order, the letters in the blue boxes give you a place name from the story. What is it?

1 Justin has a cool p r e s e n t from his dad.

2 It's a video c a m e r a.

3 A s e a g u l l takes a girl's ice cream.

4 There are lots of boats in the h a r b o u r.

5 Tom has a red T-s h i r t.

6 The boy's h a i r is brown.

7 Tom's mum is w o r r i e d.

8 Justin's mum thinks he is in t r o u b l e.

→ The place name is the Barbican.

[1] need [niːd] *brauchen*

1 PRONUNCIATION Food

WB 43 Say and match the word. Then listen and check.

1  2  3  4  5 

[ˌfruːt ˈsæləd] ['sænwɪtʃ] ['bɪskɪts] ['vedʒtəblz] [dɪ'zɜːt]

2 WORDS Home and family

a) Write and say the missing word.

1 Abby has lots of sailing trophies on the s h e l f in her bedroom.

2 In the evening, Sam's mum sits in her a r m c h a i r and reads.

3 Sam likes cornflakes with milk for b r e a k f a s t.

4 Amar is Maya's u n c l e, not her brother.

5 Lucy's uncle Jim is single. He isn't married or d i v o r c e d.

b) Match and say the phrases.

1 play	homework	4 write	a cup of tea	7 read	friends
2 watch	TV	5 feed	emails	8 meet	sailing
3 do	games	6 make	the dog	9 go	the paper

c) Take pairs from b), write five sentences in your exercise book and read them out.

3 About Nick (Simple present: positive and negative sentences)

Finish the text about Nick, Dan's best friend. Use positive and ~~negative~~ verbs.

Nick goes (go) to Plymstock with Dan. They go (go) to school at 8:15. Before school, Nick doesn't have (~~have~~) time for a big breakfast, but he takes (take) biscuits and fruit for the break. He likes (like) science and football, but he doesn't like (~~like~~) school uniforms – and Nick and Dan don't like (~~like~~) homework.

4 Your dream[1] house

Talk about your dream house. Say six to eight sentences. You can record what you say.

1 My dream house is … (near the sea/in my hometown/in Germany/in Plymouth …).
2 It has … rooms and a big … (garden/swimming pool/kitchen …).
3 I can … (swim/play games/watch TV …) every day.
4 My bedroom is … (upstairs/downstairs). It's … (yellow and blue/cool …).
5 It has lots of … (pictures/posters/shelves …).
6 There's a … and there are … in every room.

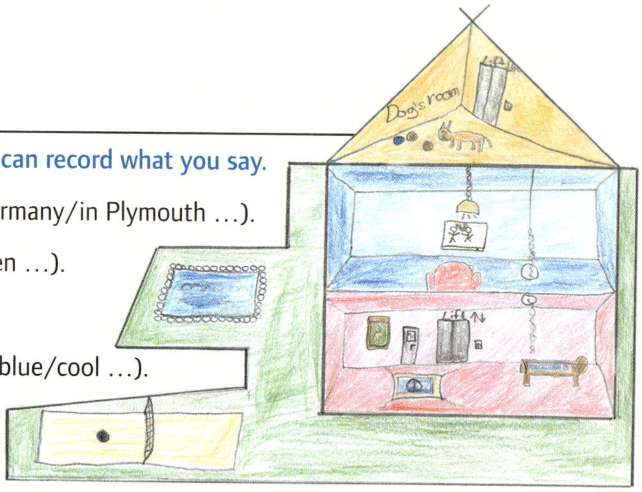

[1] dream [driːm] *Traum*

5 About you

You meet Lucy and Sam in Plymouth. Tell them about yourself. Talk for about one minute. You can record what you say. First, (circle) three things you would like to talk about:

home /family: *We have a house/flat in …, I have a brother/sister …*

school: *My school is …, I like … but I don't like …*

sports: *My favourite sport is …, I'm good at …, I play …*

animals: *I have a rabbit/cat/dog …, I feed him/her …*

after school: *After school I meet friends and we go …*

You can use the words in the box. (Circle) the words you would like to use.

nice/great/cool · science/maths/history · basketball/football · feed my dog/cat/rabbit · go for a walk · help at home · read/write emails · text/meet friends · play games · go to the shops/the park

6 Your family and friends

a) WB 44 Listen to Dan and Nina.

b) WB 45 Now answer Dan's questions about your family and friends. Nina's answers can help you. Say two or more sentences for each answer. You can record what you say.

Check: Speaking

a) Vergleiche deine Antworten mit den Lösungen auf Seite 84 im Workbook.
b) Schätze deine Antworten mit einem grünen oder roten Gesicht ein.

	🙂	☹	→
1 PRONUNCIATION Food			
Konntest du alle Wörter richtig aussprechen?	○	○	1
2 WORDS Home and family			
1 Wusstest du, welche Wörter fehlen und konntest du sie richtig aussprechen?	○	○	1, 2a–c
2 Wusstest du, welche Wörter man zusammen benutzen kann und konntest du sie in Sätzen anwenden?	○	○	2d
4 Your dream house			
Konntest du mithilfe der Vorgaben mindestens sechs Sätze zum Thema flüssig und ohne zu stocken sagen?	○	○	3
5 About you			
1 Konntest du zu deinen ausgewählten Themen mehrere Sätze bilden?	○	○	5, 6
2 Konntest du spontan und frei sprechen?	○	○	5, 6
6 Your family and friends			
1 Sind dir die Wörter für die Familienmitglieder eingefallen und konntest du sie richtig aussprechen?	○	○	2c, 6
2 Hast du die Kurzantworten richtig verwendet?	○	○	4
3 Konntest du alle Fragen über Familienangehörige/Freunde mit mindestens zwei Sätzen frei beantworten?	○	○	6

c) Wenn du dich rot eingeschätzt hast, folge den Nummern in der rechten Spalte. Sie führen dich zu den passenden Übungen im Skills Training (S. 36–37). Dort kannst du gezielt deine Sprechfertigkeiten trainieren.

1 PRONUNCIATION Say the words

WB 46 Look at the pictures. Say and write the words. Then listen and check.

TIP: You can find the words and the pronunciation in the Vocabulary in your student's book (pp. 200–218).

1 
[weɪl]
a *whale*

2 
['wʊmən]
a *woman*

3 
['kʌbəd]
a *cupboard*

4 
[bɔːd]
a *board*

5 
['bɜːθdeɪ]
a *birthday*

6 
['wɪmɪn]
two *women*

7 
[kləʊðz]
lots of *clothes*

8 
['kaːsl]
a *castle*

2 WORDS Home and family

a) WB 47 Listen. Then say and write the answers. Rooms: what is it? – It's a …

1 *kitchen*. 2 *living room*. 3 *bedroom*. 4 *dining room*.

b) WB 48 Things in your bedroom: what are they? – It's a …

1 *cupboard*. 2 *shelf*. 3 *desk*. 4 *clock*.

c) WB 49 People in your family: who are they? – … my …

1 *uncle*. 3 *aunt*. 5 *cousins*.

2 *grandfather/grandpa*. 4 *grandmother/grandma*.

d) Say four sentences with these words: 1 play games 2 watch TV 3 do homework 4 write emails.
You can use the words from 2a) and c).

3 Where are the things?

a) WB 50 Look at the pictures. Listen and answer the questions.
Say where things are. Say the room and the place:

Where's the dog's basket? – *It's in the living room on the floor.*

TIP: For longer and nicer sentences, use **phrases of place**: *in the bedroom, on the shelf, near the window, in the living room.*

b) Find a partner. Partner A asks four questions. Partner B answers the questions. Then B asks four questions and A answers them.

4 What's the best answer?

a) WB 51 Listen to the questions. Then circle and say the best answer: A, B or C.

1. A No. — **(B) No, I'm not.** — C It's nice in Plymouth.
2. A It is nice. — B Yes. — **(C) Yes, it is.**
3. A Yes. — B Yes, there are. — **(C) Yes, they are.**
4. A No. — **(B) No, there aren't.** — C They aren't.

b) WB 52 Now listen and answer four questions about yourself.

5 What can you see?

Find a partner. What can you see in the picture? Use words from the boxes. Partner A starts. Partner B repeats and adds another sentence.

A: *I can see the sea.*

B: *You can see the sea. There's a harbour.*

Then A repeats and adds another sentence.

TIP: Don't forget -s or -es with *he/she/it* in the simple present: **like → he/she/it likes.**

I can see a/two/lots of ... .
There's a ... /There are ...

café · harbour · people · sailing boats · sea · seagulls · seals · ship

6 Talk about the Plymouth kids

a) Tell an English friend about the Plymouth kids. Say three or four sentences about Justin, Maya, Mukesh, Lucy and Abby.

Sam: Sam goes to Plymstock. He has a little sister, Lily. He likes/does ... He doesn't like/eat ...

Sam	Justin	Maya	Mukesh	Lucy	Abby
Plymstock	Plymstock	Coombe Dean	Plymstock	Plymstock	Plymstock
sister: Lily	no brothers or sisters dad in Boston	brother: Mukesh	sister: Maya	sister: Holly	brother: Tim
kung fu ☺	computer games ☺	sailing ☺	computer games ☺	animals at Grandma's farm ☺	sailing ☺
vegetable soup ☹	video camera ☺	Abby's brother ☹	cricket ☹		lots of trophies

b) WB 53 Now listen and answer your English friend's questions about the Plymouth kids.

Clubs and hobbies

1 School clubs ➜ SB (pp. 68–69)

○ The names of the clubs are wrong. Find and write the correct names. Then write the name of club 6.

1 Food Club

Learn to design and make posters and cards for family and friends! Have fun too!

When: Fridays 3 pm
Where: Art room

2 Art Club

Years 7 and 8!
Learn how to make great food – yummy party food or your favourite desserts.

For girls and boys.

Mondays at 3 pm in the canteen.

5 Football Team

You like reading? Come and talk about your favourite books with other students – and get good book tips!

Library, Wed lunchtime

3 Dance Club

Years 7 and 8!
You're good with a football? You'd like to play in a team – and win?

We meet in the gym on Mondays after school.

For boys and girls.

Contact Miss Reed

4 Book Club

You're a dance fan! You'd like to learn breakdance or hip-hop? Meet us in the gym on Tuesdays at 3:10.

For girls and boys.

6 ____________

Come to our garden and help us to grow! You can take us home too! We're good for you! Contact: Mrs Green.

1 Art Club
2 Food Club
3 Football Team
4 Dance Club
5 Book Club
6 Gardening Club

2 A new club ➜ SB (pp. 68–69)

Design and make a poster for a new school club. The information in exercise 1 and the Wordbank on pp. 172–173 of your student's book can help you. You can put your poster in your My Book.
Give this information:

1 The name of your club. You can choose from the box.

2 Say what students can learn or do in your club (*act, dance, play an instrument, sing, have fun, learn how to …*).

3 Say where the club meets (*room, canteen, library, computer room, music area, school garden …*).

4 Say when the club meets (*day/time, at 3 pm, from … to … pm, after school*).

5 Maybe give the name of the teacher (*Mr …/Mrs …/Miss …*).

School Band · Film Club · Animal Club · Computer Club · Judo Club · School Disco · School Show · …

3 My club ➜ SB (pp. 68–69)

● Tell the class about your club and show your poster from exercise 2.
Say why your club is a good club. Say six or more sentences.
The class can ask questions and choose the best club.

My club is the ... Club, it's on ... at ..., it meets in ... I think it's a good club because ..., students can have fun and ... you can learn about/how to ...

4 Are you in a club? ➜ SB (p. 69)

a) WB 54 Read the sentences first. Then listen to Nina and Dan. Are the sentences right or wrong?
Circle a letter.

	Right	Wrong
1 Nina and Dan like their school clubs.	(L)	B
2 Nina is very good at tennis.	E	(A)
3 Nina is in three clubs.	(E)	A
4 Dan doesn't like tennis.	A	(T)
5 Plymstock doesn't have a tennis club.	(O)	K
6 Charlotte loves football.	(I)	B
7 Charlotte doesn't play in a football team.	S	(N)
8 Nina and Charlotte like the Science Club.	(P)	T
9 Dan is in the Basketball Club.	(R)	B
10 Dan is in the Food Club and the Science Club too.	L	(M)

b) In the right order, the letters in a) give you the name of a Plymstock club.

➜ It's the T r a m p o l i n e Club.

5 Does Justin tell jokes? (Simple present: questions) ➜ SB (p. 72)

Ask about the persons in brackets ( ).

1 Sam tells jokes. (Justin?) Does Justin tell jokes?

2 Justin has a camera. (Lucy?) Does Lucy have a camera?

3 Abby goes sailing. (Sam and Lucy?) Do Sam and Lucy go sailing?

4 Maya knows Abby. (Lucy?) Does Lucy know Abby?

5 Sam plays basketball. (Lucy and Maya?) Do Lucy and Maya play basketball?

6 Abby goes to the Trampoline Club. (Sam?) Does Sam go to the Trampoline Club?

7 Justin likes film making. (you?) Do you like film making?

8 Abby lives in Wembury. (Maya and Lucy?) Do Maya and Lucy live in Wembury?

6 Holly and Lucy (Simple present: questions and short answers) ➜ SB (p. 72)

a) ○ Finish Holly's questions with do or does. Then write Lucy's answers.

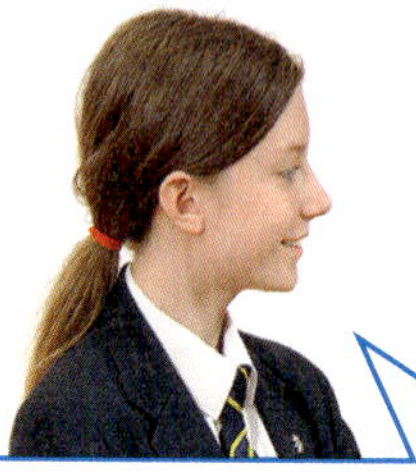

	Holly		Lucy
1	Do	students in the Gardening Club meet every day?	No, they don't.
2	Does	Abby go to the Trampoline Club?	Yes, she does.
3	Does	the Film Making Club meet on Tuesdays?	No, it doesn't.
4	Do	Abby and Maya go to Wembury Sailing Club?	Yes, they do.
5	Does	Sam go to the Film Making Club?	No, he doesn't.
6	Do	you go to the Samba Club?	No, I don't.

b) ● Write four questions with do or does about the Plymouth kids and their families.

Do the Sens live in Wembury? Does Mukesh like cricket?

1 ____

2 ____

3 ____

4 ____

c) Ask a partner your questions. Your partner has to answer with short answers. Take turns.

7 WORDS Sports and activities ➜ SB (p. 72)

Look at the pictures and write the correct words. Then find and write the word in the blue boxes.

2

3

1

4

5

6

7

8

				↓					
1				c	a	r	d	s	
2			y	o	g	a			
3	d	r	u	m	s				
4				p	i	a	n	o	
5			j	u	d	o			
6	s	k	a	t	i	n	g		
7		c	h	e	s	s			
8				r	i	d	i	n	g

➜ This club is always good! It's the C o m p u t e r Club.

8 WORDS Sam plays basketball ➜ SB (p. 73)

Finish the sentences with a form of *go*, *play* or *do*.

1 Sam *plays* basketball.
2 Do Abby and Maya *go* sailing?
3 Does Sam *do* kung fu?
4 Who can *play* chess?
5 Maya *goes* swimming.
6 Do Lucy and Holly *play* tennis?
7 Who *does* yoga?
8 Who *plays* the drums?

9 MIXED BAG Free time (simple present + *go/play/do*) ➜ SB (p. 73)

Put in the missing words.

Maya: Your sister and my brother *are* in Year 9 at Plymstock. *Does* Holly know Mukesh?

Lucy: I *don't* know. I *can* ask her. Maybe they *go* to the same club. Holly is in the Computer Games Club.

Maya: Oh! Mukesh *goes* to the Computer Games Club too. He *plays/loves* silly computer games.

Lucy: I *don't* like computer games. Holly *does* gymnastics, and I think she *does* judo too.

Maya: Mukesh *doesn't* like cricket but he sometimes *plays* football with his friends. And what about you, Lucy? Which clubs *do* you like? I know that you *don't* want to *join* the Science Club.

Lucy: Right. But the Samba Club *sounds* fun. What about you? You*'re* in the Wembury Sailing Club, right? *Does* Abby *go* sailing with you?

Maya: Yes, *she does*. She's nice. But *you* are my best friend, Lucy.

10 Who has to do what? (*have to*) ➜ SB (p. 73)

Dan's mum is not at home this week. Here is a 'to do' list for Dan and his sister Gemma. Write sentences.

To do! Don't forget!
1 clean the kitchen - G
2 clean the bathroom - D
3 visit Grandma - G & D
4 feed Charlie - D
5 choose a present for Grandpa's birthday - G&D
6 make some biscuits - D
7 do your homework! - G&D!!

1 *Gemma has to clean the kitchen.*
2 *Dan has to clean the bathroom.*
3 *Gemma and Dan have to visit Grandma.*
4 *Dan has to feed Charlie.*
5 *Gemma and Dan have to choose a present for Grandpa's birthday.*
6 *Dan has to make some biscuits.*
7 *Gemma and Dan have to do their homework.*

11 STUDY SKILLS Collecting information (Making a table) ➜ SB (p. 74)

a) ● WB 55 Listen to Nina and her friends. Put the information about their clubs in Nina's table. Then listen again and check.

	clubs and activities	day	time
Nina	Science Club Reading Tennis	Tuesdays Mondays Thursdays	3–4 lunchtime 3–4:30
Emily	Chess	Fridays	lunchtime
Dan	Food	Mondays	after school
	Basketball	Thursdays	3–4:30
Charlotte	Football	Wednesdays	after school
	Science	Tuesdays	3–4
Amira	Chess	Fridays	lunchtime

b) When do they all have time to meet? They all have time to meet on Friday after school.

12 Guess who (Simple present: questions with question words) ➜ SB (p. 77)

a) You ask one of the Plymouth kids questions. Read the answers. Then write your questions with the correct question word from the box and do or does.

How · What · When · Where · Why

1 When does your first lesson start?	It starts at 9 o'clock.
2 How do you go to school?	I ride my bike.
3 Where do you have lunch?	We have lunch in the school canteen.
4 When does school end?	It ends at 3 o'clock.
5 What do you do on Saturdays?	I meet my friends and I go to the Lido.
6 What school club do you go to?	I go to the Basketball Club.
7 When does your club meet?	It meets on Thursdays from 3 to 4:30.
8 Where does the club meet?	The club meets in the gym.
9 Why do you play basketball?	I play basketball because I like team games.
10 What hobbies do you have?	Well, my favourite hobby is kung fu.

b) Who is it in a)? Write the student's name and finish the sentence.

The student is Sam. I know this because he goes to the Basketball Club/he's in the Basketball Club and his favourite hobby is kung fu.

1 GB and the UK ➔ SB (pp. 42–43)

a) This is Morph's text. Put in the missing words. One statement is wrong. Can you find it?

'GB' is short for *Great Britain*, that's England, *Scotland* and *Wales*. The *capital* of England is Plymouth, oh no, sorry. That *isn't right*. It's London. Yes, yes. There are *people* from lots of *different* countries there. Scotland is a great *country* with a great history. Five *million* people live there. The capital is *Edinburgh*. In Wales, people speak English, but students learn *Welsh* in school too. *Cardiff*, the capital, is famous *for* its old castle and many other sights. 'UK' is short for the *United Kingdom*. *Northern* Ireland is part of the UK too. *Belfast* is the capital. It's a *port*, so you can see big *ships* there, and the *famous* monster Nessie too. Come to the UK in *summer* when it's warm. There are lots of great places and things to see.

b) You can go to the UK for two weeks. What can you see and do there? Write four sentences in your exercise book.

2 Special days ➔ SB (pp. 66–67)

a) Write the missing words in the puzzle. What's the word down?

1 Christmas and birthdays are … days.
2 You write … for your family and friends.
3 24th December is Christmas …
4 On your birthday you have a cake and you can make a …
5 In the UK people eat roast … for Christmas dinner.
6 British kids have … on their birthday cakes.
7 They often give party … to their friends.

							↓					
1						s	p	e	c	i	a	l
2					c	a	r	d	s			
3							E	v	e			
4					w	i	s	h				
5			t	u	r	k	e	y				
6					c	a	n	d	l	e	s	
7	i	n	v	i	t	a	t	i	o	n	s	

b) ● Christmas or birthdays, what do you like best? Why? Write three sentences.

I like … best because …

3 Shopping → SB (pp. 92–93)

a) WB 72 Listen to Sarah and the shop assistant.
Then write answers to questions 1–6. Read the questions before you listen.

1 What does Sarah want to look at in the shop? *T-shirts.*

2 What size does she want? *L.*

3 Why is size M too small? *The T-shirt is for her big brother.*

4 What colour would she like? *Red.*

5 Does the assistant have a red T-shirt in size L? *Yes, she does.*

6 What does Sarah take? *A dark blue T-shirt in L.*

b) You are in a shoe shop with your English friend Luke. He needs some new trainers but he can't speak German. He and the shop assistant need your help. Say only what is important. Don't translate.

Assistant: Welche Größe braucht dein Freund?

You (to Luke): *She says what size do you want.*

Luke: I don't know. Maybe 5 or 5½. Or 6? UK, European and US sizes are different.

You (to assistant): *Er meint vielleicht 5 oder 6.*

Assistant: Wir können ein paar verschiedene Größen probieren. Welche Farbe gefällt deinem Freund?

You (to Luke): *She says you can try different sizes. What colour do you want?*

Luke: A dark colour. You don't have to clean dark shoes so often.

You (to assistant): *Er möchte dunkle Schuhe.*

Assistant: OK. Dann probieren wir erst mal diesen Schuh. Schauen wir, ob die Größe passt.

You (to Luke): *Try this size. Is it OK?*

Luke: No, it's too small. Does she have the next size? I like the trainers but I don't like the colour.

You (to assistant): *Sie sind zu klein, aber sie gefallen ihm. Haben Sie die nächste Größe? Und welche anderen Farben gibt es?*

Assistant: OK. Das ist jetzt 39. Es gibt sie in Schwarz mit Grau, Blau mit Weiß oder Schwarz mit Gelb.

You (to Luke): *She has these shoes in black and grey, blue and white or black and yellow.*

Luke: OK. Black and grey.

You (to assistant): *Schwarz mit Grau.*

Assistant: Ja, OK. Schwarz mit Grau. Und hier ist der zweite Schuh. Er kann beide probieren.

You (to Luke): *Try the other shoe too.*

Luke: They look cool. I hope they're big enough. Oh, yes. They're good. How do they look? How much are they?

You (to assistant): *Was kosten sie?*

Assistant: Moment bitte. 46,90.

You (to Luke): *Forty-six ninety.*

Luke: Oh, OK, but I hope I have enough euros.

c) ● Write a shopping dialogue with a partner.

4 London ➜ *SB (pp. 118–119)*

a) Complete the text.

London is the *capital* of England. It's a big *city* on the River Thames where people from all countries of the *world* live and work. The city has 17 *million* visitors every year. Buckingham *Palace*, the home of *Queen* Elizabeth II, the Tower of London, the Houses of *Parliament* and Big Ben are favourite places. London also has some famous *churches* like St. Paul's Cathedral and Westminster Abbey. London is an exciting place to visit – and to learn English.

b) ● WB 73 Listen twice. Which photo of London streets does the speaker describe? Circle A, B, C or D.

A

C

B

D

b) Choose one of the other three photos and describe it. Use: There is/are …, We can see …, on the right/left, in the foreground/middle/background; behind, in front of, next to. Write in your exercise book. Read your text to a partner. Can he or she guess which photo your text describes?

5 The USA and Canada → SB (pp. 144–145)

a) Choose a place in the USA or Canada where tourists often go. Ideas: a city, a national park (the Everglades, the Rocky Mountains) or a famous sight (the White House).

1 Collect information (from the internet, magazines, family and friends) about your place.

2 Make a poster with pictures, captions, a title and sub-title, short texts with important information.

3 Show the poster to your group and give a one-minute talk about your place. Describe your picture(s). Say what's in the picture. Say what people are doing. Your talk must be interesting and easy to understand. Give information about your place: say where it is, what you can see and do there, why you would like to go there. You can use these phrases:

My talk is about ... It is/has/was ... In the picture(s) you can see ...
I think it is interesting for tourists because ..., People/Visitors go there because ...
I would like to visit ... because I think ...

b) Look at the pictures. In your group, talk about what and where they are. Then tell the rest of the class about it.

I think that's ... because there's/there are ..., That must be ... It's in ...

6 English as a world language → SB (pp. 146–147)

a) ● Complete the text.

The countries where people speak English are: *the UK and Ireland, the USA, Canada, Australia and New Zealand*.

In *India* and *South Africa* English is an *official* language.

b) You hear, speak, read and write English in school. How can this help you in your free time? The text in your student's book (pp. 144–145) can help you. Add your own ideas.

1 You can have friends in lots of countries.

2 ______

3 ______

4 ______

5 ______

13 Questions for a friend (Simple present: mixed questions) ➜ SB (p. 78)

Lucy wants to write an email to a new friend. What can she ask?
Start with do/does or with a question word. Exercise 10 can help you.

Lucy: Now I have some questions for you.

1 Where – live? *Where do you live?*

2 have – any brothers or sisters? *Do you have any brothers or sisters?*

3 Where – go – school? *Where do you go to school?*

4 When – school – start and finish? *When does school start and finish?*

5 have clubs – school? *Does your school have clubs?*

6 What – in your free time – do? *What do you do in your free time?*

7 What music – like? *What music do you like?*

8 Where – with your friends – go? *Where do you go with your friends?*

14 An email ➜ SB (p. 78)

● On the computer, write an email to Lucy, Maya, Abby, Justin or Sam. In your email, write about you and ask five or more questions about their school, clubs, family, free time … Exercises 6, 12 and 13 of this Workbook unit can help you. You can put your email in your My Book.

Hi Abby/Sam …!
Your school and your clubs sound nice. I … Do you …?
Does your brother/sister …? What do you do …?

15 REVISION PRONUNCIATION What can you hear? ➜ SB (p. 78)

WB 56 Listen and mark what you hear. Then listen again and check.

1 **work** / walk	4 **hair** / hear	7 to / **too**
2 **choose** / shoes	5 later / **letter**	8 Tim / **team**
3 we're / **wear**	6 **age** / H	9 **year** / your

16 Who knows Abby? (Subject and object questions) ➔ SB (p. 79)

Read the answers and write the questions. Where do you need do or does? Look at the underlined sentence parts for help.

1 *Who knows Abby?* — Maya knows Abby.

2 *Who does Morph know?* — Morph knows all the Plymouth kids.

3 *Who tells silly jokes?* — Sam tells silly jokes.

4 *Who likes film making?* — Justin likes film making.

5 *What does Justin film?* — Justin films the harbour.

6 *Who goes to the Trampoline Club?* — Abby goes to the Trampoline Club.

7 *Who does Abby like?* — Abby likes Maya.

8 *What does Morph do every day?* — Morph reads and sleeps every day.

17 Silky's party (Object pronouns) ➔ SB (p. 79)

Finish the dialogue with: me, you, her, him, it, us, them.

Remember:
When German 'sie' is an object pronoun, it can be **her** or **it** or **them**!

1 Where's Silky? Can you see **her**?

2 Where's the list? Can you see **it**?

3 Where are the sharks[1]? Can you see **them**?

Silky: Now, where are the invitations to my party? I can't find *them*.

Spot: Oh? A party? Is there an invitation for *me*, Silky?

Silky: Of course there's an invitation for *you*, Spot. You're my friend. We're good friends. I like *you* and you like *me*.

Spot: And what about Sherman? Is there an invitation for *him* too?

Silky: Yes, there is. But not for his big brothers! I don't like *them*.

Spot: And they don't like *us*. They just want to eat *us*! But what about Octavia? You like *her*.

Silky: Yes, Octavia is nice. She can come, of course. We all like *her*. And Sydney. We all like *him*. His friends are nice too. I like *them* all.

Spot: What about Uncle Wilbur? Do you like *him*?

Silky: Uncle Wilbur? Well, erm … Oh, look! There's my list.

Spot: Can I see *it*, please, Silky? Mmmm. But where's Uncle Wilbur's name? I can't find *it* on your list. Is it because he always eats too much?

[1] shark [ʃɑːk] *Hai*

18 Amira and Ranjiv ➔ SB (p. 79)

a) ○ Read what Amira says.

Hi! My name is Amira, and this is my brother Ranjiv. I'm 11 and Ranjiv is 13.

My friends are Nina and Emily. We all go to Coombe Dean. It's a nice school. I really like maths and ICT, they're my best subjects. I don't like English, but that's Ranjiv's favourite subject. He doesn't like art. We love sports. I play tennis and Ranjiv is in the football team. I like basketball too.

My hobbies are reading and music. I play the drums and Ranjiv plays the guitar. We aren't very good, but it's fun. Ranjiv often plays chess with Dad, but Dad always wins. Oh, we have some animals at home too. Ranjiv has a guinea pig, Honey, and Hector is my rabbit. I'd like a cat too.

b) Finish the table about Amira and Ranjiv. Collect this information: age, school, likes …, doesn't like …, sports, hobbies/free time, animals.

	age	school	likes	doesn't like	sports	hobbies/ free time	animals
Amira	*11*	*Coombe Dean*	*maths, ICT*	*English*	*tennis, basketball*	*reading, drums*	*rabbit*
Ranjiv	*13*	*Coombe Dean*	*English*	*art*	*football*	*guitar, chess*	*guinea pig*

c) ● Write a profile (6–7 sentences) of Amira or Ranjiv in your exercise book. Use information from your table.

Amira is eleven years old. She's a student at … Her favourite …
Ranjiv is … He's a …

19 REVISION WORDS Find pairs ➔ SB (p. 79)

○ Find and write pairs.

after · always · before · behind · big · cold · downstairs · hot · in front of · loud · never · old · quiet · small · upstairs · young

big – small | *cold – hot* | *downstairs – upstairs*

always – never | *loud – quiet* | *behind – in front of*

old – young | *before – after*

20 Open day at the sports centre ➔ *SB (p. 82)*

You are in town with your American cousin. When you see this poster at the sports centre, your cousin wants to know what it says. Answer the questions in English.

TIP: Read the questions first. Find the information you need and underline it. Don't translate. Give short answers with words you know.

Tag der offenen Tür
Samstag, 10. April, ab 10:30 Uhr
Eintritt frei!

Sportbegeisterte und Neugierige sind herzlich eingeladen, unser Sportangebot in den vielen verschiedenen Abteilungen auszuprobieren: z. B. Gymnastik, Kinderturnen, Badminton, Fußball, Klettern, Trampolin, Karate u. v. m.
Unsere Trainer und Trainerinnen stehen Ihnen mit Rat und Tat zur Seite. Informieren Sie sich an unseren Infoständen! Schauen Sie zu oder machen Sie bei unseren Spielen mit!
Es gibt Preise, Probestunden und Trikots zu gewinnen.

Hier einige Highlights aus unserem Programm:
- Fußballjugendturnier
- Show-Tennis
- Karatevorführung
- Bambini-Fußball
- Trampolinvorführung
- Gymnastikvorführung
- Torwandschießen
- Show-Tanzkids
- Tischtennisturnier

Neben einem attraktiven Rahmenprogramm wird im Restaurant für das leibliche Wohl gesorgt:
ganztags warme Küche, Getränke sowie Snacks und Grillspezialitäten im Freien.
Info, Spaß und Spiel für die ganze Familie!

1 What's that poster about?
2 When does it start and how much are tickets?
3 What is there for kids?
4 What can you win?
5 Can I try the climbing wall?
6 What is there to eat?

21 What's correct? (Possessive forms) ➔ *SB (p. 82)*

Write sentences 1–8 again. Use -'s, -s' or of with the words in brackets ( ). You can change the order.

1 (film – Justin) is about the Barbican. — *Justin's film is about the Barbican.*
2 What's the (museum – name) in the Barbican? — *What's the name of the museum in the Barbican?*
3 The (house – rooms) are small and dark. — *The rooms of the house are small and dark.*
4 What happens at (film – end)? — *What happens at the end of the film?*
5 The (house – Blackwells) is in Wembury. — *The Blackwells' house is in Wembury.*
6 The Blackwells have a dog. The (name - dog) is Skip. — *The dog's name is Skip.*
7 Abby has a cat too. The (cat – name) is Mink. — *The cat's name is Mink.*
8 (house – Abby) is near the (end – road). — *Abby's house is near the end of the road.*

22 SPELLING small or Capital letters? ➜ SB (p. 83)

There are 20 more spelling mistakes with small and capital letters in Morph's text.

a) ○ Read his text and mark the wrong letters.

b) Write Morph's text again in your exercise book and correct his mistakes.

My Name is morph. i live in the library at plymstock school. It's a very nice School in plymouth – a big Town in england. You can learn english from the english Books in my library. There are lots of Clubs at our school. I'm in the quiet reading club. It meets from monday to friday at Lunchtime. In august it's very, very quiet in my library, and there's only me in my club – because the Students aren't there.

23 Morph never does homework (Word order: adverbs of frequency) ➜ SB (p. 83)

a) One adverb in each sentence is in the wrong place. ~~Cross~~ it out.
Write correct sentences in your exercise book.

1 Morph never does ~~never~~ homework.
2 Sam often tells ~~often~~ silly jokes.
3 Abby ~~always~~ doesn't always go sailing on Sundays.
4 Lucy usually meets Maya ~~usually~~ at the Broadway.
5 Justin sometimes films ~~sometimes~~ seals and seagulls.
6 Sam ~~often~~ doesn't often go on the Big Wheel.

b) Write correct sentences.

1 the kids · in town · meet · often — The kids often meet in town.
2 aren't · on the Hoe · they · always — They aren't always on the Hoe.
3 take · their bikes · sometimes · they · to a park — They sometimes take their bikes to a park.
4 don't · go skating · they · usually — They don't usually go skating.
5 is · often · Justin · on Saturdays · at the harbour — Justin is often at the harbour on Saturdays.

c) ● In your exercise book, write four sentences about you, with:
1: always, 2: not often, 3: never, 4: not usually.

24 SPELLING What's correct? (The plural of nouns) ➜ SB (p. 84)

Write the plural forms in the correct list.

class · crab · box · diary · dictionary · half · hobby · life · language · lunch · monkey · shelf · toy · trophy · way

–s	–es [-ɪz]	–ies	–ves
crabs	classes	diaries	halves
monkeys	boxes	dictionaries	lives
toys	languages	hobbies	shelves
ways	lunches	trophies	

25 MIXED BAG Sam and Maya ➜ SB (p. 84)

Put in the missing word(s).

Sam: Lucy *says* that you're a good swimmer, Maya. *Do* you often *go* swimming?

Maya: Yes, I *do*. I love *it*. I *go* sailing with Abby too. All the Blackwells like sailing. It's *their* favourite sport. *They're* at the sailing club every Sunday. Sailing is fun, but you *have to* practise. What's your favourite sport, Sam?

Sam: *My* favourite sport? Well, I *do* kung fu and I *play* basketball. I like ball games.

Maya: I *don't* play ball games. I like water sports. What about Justin? What *does* he do?

Sam: Justin is cool. I like *him*. He has some cool *hobbies*, like film making. He *wants* to make a film of Plymouth for *his* dad in Boston. You can see *us* three in the film too, *me*, you and Lucy.

Maya: Really? We're all in it? *Who* does what? And what's the name *of* the film?

Sam: It *doesn't* have a name. And Lucy? What's *her* favourite hobby? *Does* she play an instrument?

Maya: Yes, she *does*. She *goes* to piano lessons. She *can* sing too. And what about your friends in London, Sam. Do you text *them*?

Sam: Oh, yes. We talk every week too. I have to *tell* them my new jokes!

26 Pronunciation course [f, v, w] ➜ SB (p. 85)

a) WB 57 Listen and practise words with a [v]-sound.

very · over · travel · interview · every · visit · activity · never

b) WB 58 Listen and practise words with a [w]-sound.

wake up · walk · water · why · wear · warm · word · when · wet

c) WB 59 Listen and repeat the phrases with [v]-, [w]- and [f]-sounds. You can record your voice.

1 who, what, where, when and why?
2 a warm, wet and windy week
3 visit a farm in Wales
4 watch five very funny videos
5 four favourite vegetables

d) WB 60 Say the words. Where is the stressed syllable? Write the words in the correct list. Then listen and check.

afternoon · canteen · *cousin* · dessert · information · programme · salad · technology

1st syllable	2nd syllable	3rd syllable
cousin	*canteen*	*afternoon*
programme	*dessert*	*information*
salad	*technology*	

27 TEXT The captain's ghost ➜ SB (pp. 86–87)

a) ○ People in the story. Who is it? Write the correct names. For help look at pp. 86–87 in your student's book.

1 *May* and *Abigail* go to the attic.

2 *Skipper* has a book in his mouth.

3 *Captain Justin Pascoe* is the name in the diary.

4 *Lucille* lives in New Street.

5 The boy's name is *Samuel*.

6 *May* and *Abigail* want to help Lucille.

7 The ghost is *Captain Justin Pascoe*.

8 *Lucille* finds her father's gold.

9 Lucille gives *May* a gold coin.

10 The ghost story is *Lucy*'s dream.

b) Match and write the correct sentences under the pictures.
Then put the pictures in the right order. Write 1–4 in the boxes.

Captain Pascoe's gold is there!

This can't be Plymouth. Where are we?

It's a letter from a girl.

Is it Lucille's father?

Who are they?

What's that in May's hand?

4

What's that in May's hand?

1

It's a letter from a girl.

2

Who are they?

3

Captain Pascoe's gold is there!

c) ● Answer the questions. Write two or more sentences for each question.

1 Do you like the story? (*time travellers, ghost, great, boring, scary, silly*)

Yes, I do. I think it's ... Not really. I don't ...

2 Do you think it's a good story for a film (*good idea, history, time travellers, the Barbican, old houses, dream, ghost, fight, gold, great, scary, silly*)? *I like/don't like ... You can/can't show ...*

1 WORDS Can you spell it?

WB 61 Listen and write.

1 skating
2 edit
3 riding
4 guitar
5 drums
6 bike
7 chocolate
8 idea

2 Silky and Morph

Write correct sentences.

1 crabs – for breakfast – have – Silky – does

Does Silky have crabs for breakfast?

2 does – where – with her friends – Silky – swim?

Where does Silky swim with her friends?

3 usually – doesn't – in the Lido pool – Silky – swim

Silky doesn't usually swim in the Lido pool.

4 books – does – what – read – Morph?

What books does Morph read?

5 reads – Morph – often – about ghosts – stories

Morph often reads stories about ghosts.

3 Plymstock clubs

a) Collect information about three clubs. Write the club names in the table. Then add the correct information.

Music area
Mon to Fri lunchtime
With Mr Willis
Library
Thurs 3–4 pm
Mon lunchtime
FILM MAKING
TE9
SAMBA CLUB
QUIET READING
Learn about good books for young people.
With Mr Wood
With Mrs Hart
You can dance, sing or play an instrument?
Learn to edit videos on the computer.

Clubs	Where?	When?	Teacher	What you do
1 Samba	Music area	Mon lunchtime	Mr Willis	dance, sing, play an instrument
2 Quiet Reading	Library	Mon to Fri lunchtime	Mr Wood	learn about good books for young people
3 Film Making	TE9	Thurs 3–4 pm	Mrs Hart	learn to edit videos on the computer

b) Your favourite club from a) needs more students. Write a text for a big club poster with information from your table in your exercise book. Make your club sound fun too! Write six or more sentences.

Ideas: *Is it sometimes boring at lunchtime/after school? Do you like ...? Can you ...? Come and ... You can learn ... is cool!*

Join the Quiet Reading Club! You can read my favourite scary stories!

4 About Leo ✎

a) WB 62 Read the mini-poster of Leo's profile. Some things are wrong. Listen to Leo and Emily and correct the mistakes.

Name: Leo Cooper	
Age: ~~11~~	*12*
School: ~~Coombe Dean~~	*Plymstock*
Class: 7~~AJ~~	*AG*
Family: ~~a brother~~	*two sisters*
Animals: ~~a dog~~ Arnold	*a rabbit*
Friends: Nina and ~~Noah~~	*Nick*
School subjects: ☺ art, ~~ICT~~	*science*
☹ maths, ~~music~~	*French*
School clubs: Gardening Club, ~~Science~~ Club	*Samba*
Sports: ~~sailing~~	*skating, riding his bike*
Hobbies: ~~plays the piano,~~ makes model ships, watches TV	*plays the drums/guitar*
Favourite music: hip hop, ~~rock~~	*rap*

b) Write a correct text about Leo in complete sentences in your exercise book. Use **and**, **but** and **because** to make your text nice.

Leo is 12 years old and he goes to Plymstock School ...

Check: Writing

a) Vergleiche deine Antworten mit den Lösungen auf Seite 84 im Workbook.
b) Schätze deine Antworten mit einem grünen oder roten Gesicht ein.

	☺	☹	
1 WORDS Can you spell it? Konntest du die Wörter richtig schreiben?	○	○	➔ 1
2 Silky and Morph			
1 Konntest du Fragen mit *question word* + *do/does* richtig bilden?	○	○	➔ 3b
2 Konntest du *adverbs of frequency* (*always*, *usually*) an die richtige Stelle im Satz platzieren?	○	○	➔ 2a + b
3 Plymstock clubs			
1 Konntest du die Informationen richtig in der Tabelle unterbringen?	○	○	➔ 5a
2 Konntest du in deinem Postertext passende Informationen aus der Tabelle benutzen?	○	○	➔ 5b
3 Konntest du in deinem Postertext Fragen (z. B. mit *Can/Do* ...) richtig stellen?	○	○	➔ 3a
4 About Leo Konntest du in deinem Text einige Sätze mit *and*, *but* und *because* verbinden?	○	○	➔ 4a + b

c) Wenn du dich rot eingeschätzt hast, schau dir die rechte Spalte an. Die Nummern führen dich zu den passenden Übungen im Skills Training (S. 52–53). Dort kannst du gezielt Schreiben trainieren.

1 WORDS Spelling

Label the picture.

1 
guitar

2 
bike

3 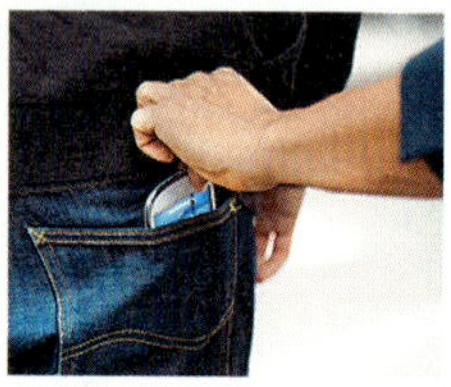
thief

4 
skates

5 
chocolate

2 How often (Adverbs of frequency)

a) Write the sentences with the word in brackets ( ) in the right place.

1 Do seals eat fish and crabs? (always)

Do seals always eat fish and crabs?

2 Morph reads books about spelling. (never)

Morph never reads books about spelling.

3 Silky doesn't sleep all day. (usually)

Silky doesn't usually sleep all day.

4 Morph doesn't clean his bookshelves. (often)

Morph doesn't often clean his bookshelves.

b) Write about yourself. Choose: sometimes, never, (don't) usually, (don't) always, (don't) often.

1 I ____________ get up at lunchtime.

2 I ____________ ride my bike in the living room.

3 I ____________ forget my homework.

TIP: Put *adverbs of frequency*
– **before** the main verb
– **after** *don't/doesn't*
– **after** a form of *be*.

3 What about the others? (Questions)

a) Write questions about the persons in brackets ( ).

TIP: Look at the verb in the statement! Start your questions with *Is/Are …? / Can …? / Do/Does …?*

1 Charlotte **likes** parties. (Emily?) Does Emily like parties too?

2 Nina **can** dance. (you?) Can you dance too?

3 Leo **plays** the drums. (you?) Do you play the drums too?

4 Charlotte **is** good at football. (Amira and Nina?) Are Amira and Nina good at football too?

5 Dan **goes** to the Food Club. (Nick?) Does Nick go to the Food Club too?

b) Read Nick's answers. Then write the questions. Start with a question word.

TIP: Remember the order:
1 question word
2 *do/does*
3 subject (here: you)
4 infinitive of main verb (*do, meet, go*).

Questions	Nick's answers
1 What do you do in your free time, Nick?	I often meet my friends.
2 When do you meet your friends?	I usually meet them in the afternoon.
3 Where do you go?	I go to the park.
4 What do you do there?	We sometimes play football.

4 Justin can't go because …

TIP: When you join two sentences, don't change the order of the words.

a) Match sentences from A and B with **and**, **but** or **because**.

A

1 Justin can't go to the Basketball Club.
2 Abby is in the Trampoline Club.
3 Lucy doesn't want to join the Science Club.
4 Maya doesn't play the piano.
5 Sam can't go to kung fu.

B

She doesn't want more school work.
His Film Making Club is at the same time.
She's in Wembury Sailing Club.
He has to help his dad.
She plays the guitar.

1 *Justin can't go to the Basketball Club because his Film Making Club is at the same time.*

2 *Abby is in the Trampoline Club and she's in Wembury Sailing Club.*

3 *Lucy doesn't want to join the Science Club because she doesn't want more school work.*

4 *Maya doesn't play the piano, but she plays the guitar.*

5 *Sam can't go to kung fu because he has to help his dad.*

b) Write three sentences about yourself: 1 with **and**, 2 with **but**, 3 with **because**.

1 ______

2 ______

3 ______

5 A party

a) WB 63 Listen to Nina, Dan, Charlotte and Emily. Then write the correct information in the table.

	Nina	Dan	Charlotte	Emily
Where?	*at the Hoe*	*in his garden*	*in the park*	*at the beach*
When?	*on Sat evening*	*on Sat afternoon*	*on Fri after school*	*on Sun afternoon*
Food? What can they make?	*pizza*	*biscuits*	*sandwiches and salad*	*a chocolate dessert*
Activities? What do they want to do?	*dance, play cool music*	*play games, watch a DVD*	*make a party film*	*have a team quiz*

b) Write a text about the four students with information from the table in your exercise book.

Nina wants to have the party at the Hoe on Saturday evening. She can make pizza. She wants to dance and play cool music. Dan wants …

Weekends

tneo
zngmaaaei
flei stcajke
rntiasre
ttionniiva
ettlob
htsros
lbomie eohnps

1 WORDS What is it? ➜ SB (pp. 94–95)

Finish the sentences with correct words from the boxes.

1 Abby, Maya and Tim want to go sailing. Their things are ready: three *life jackets*, a map, some chocolate, a big *bottle* of water and their *mobile phones*.

2 Sam has a basketball game on Saturday: Plymstock – Devonport. The Plymstock School sports kit is a black T-shirt and black *shorts*. Sam also has some very nice basketball *trainers*.

3 On her birthday, Lucy wants to go on the Wheel of Plymouth with her friends. She has a 'Welcome to Plymouth' *magazine* on her desk.

4 Silky and Spot find a *note* in an old bottle. It's an *invitation* to a seals' party next Sunday.

2 WORDS Places to go ➜ SB (pp. 94–95)

a) (Circle) and write eight more places to go on Saturdays.

c	l	i	b	r	a	r	y	p
a	s	m	u	s	e	u	m	a
f	z	h	l	a	k	e	o	r
é	o	c	l	u	b	p	p	k
i	o	n	g	g	y	m	*	m
a	l	c	i	n	e	m	a	l

↓
café
zoo
park

→
library
museum
lake
club
gym
cinema

b) The other letters tell you where Lucy and Maya often go on Saturdays.

→ It's the *s h o p p i n g m a l l*.

3 My Sundays ➜ SB (p. 95)

● Class 7EB's English homework is: 'My Sundays'. Do the homework too in your exercise book. Write six or more sentences about where you go and what you do on Sundays.

Use: In the morning/afternoon/evening, sometimes, often, usually, …
The places in exercise 2 can help you.

Sundays are sometimes boring/exciting/… so I often … In the morning I always …

4 Where were they last Saturday? (Simple past: *be*) ➔ *SB (p. 97)*

a) Look at the photos and say where the students were.

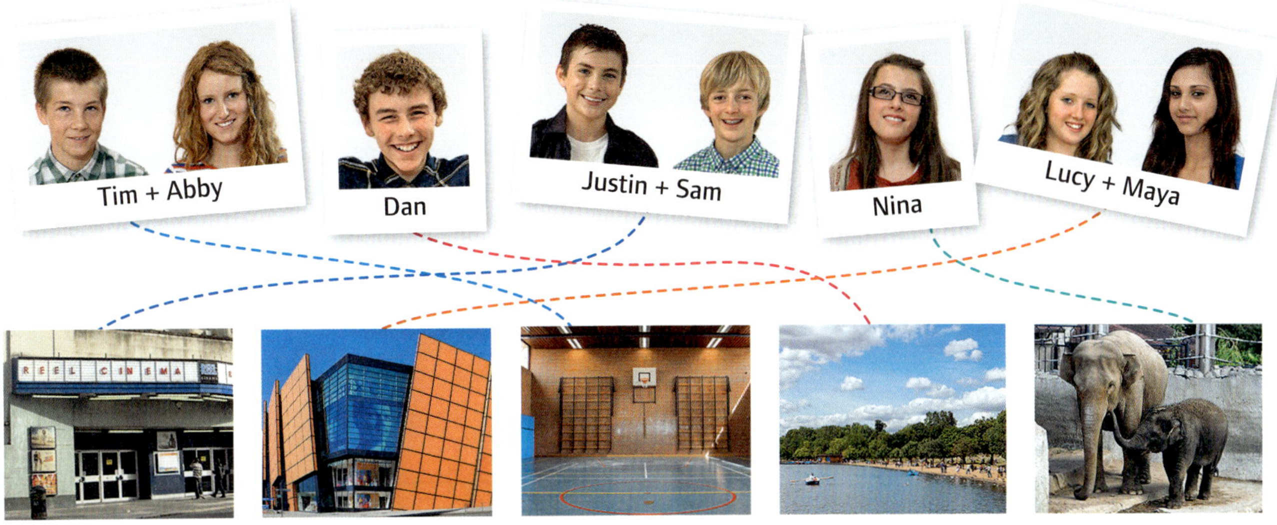

b) Now write questions and give short answers.

1 Tim and Abby/at the zoo? *Were Tim and Abby at the zoo? – No, they weren't. They were at the gym.*

2 Dan/at a lake? *Was Dan at a lake? – Yes, he was.*

3 Justin and Sam/at the cinema? *Were Justin and Sam at the cinema? – Yes, they were.*

4 Nina/at the shopping mall? *Was Nina at the shopping mall? – No, she wasn't. She was at the zoo.*

5 Lucy and Maya/at the gym? *Were Lucy and Maya at the gym? – No, they weren't.*

They were at the shopping mall.

c) ● Where were you last Saturday morning, afternoon and evening? Write three sentences.

Last Saturday morning I was ... In the afternoon my friend and I were ...

1 ______________________________

2 ______________________________

3 ______________________________

d) Ask your partner three questions about last Saturday. The questions in b) can help you. Your partner has to answer. Take turns.

[1]shark [ˈʃɒːk] *Hai*

5 Find the forms (Simple past: regular verbs) ➜ SB (p. 100)

○ Find and colour the verbs in the snake and write them in the simple past.

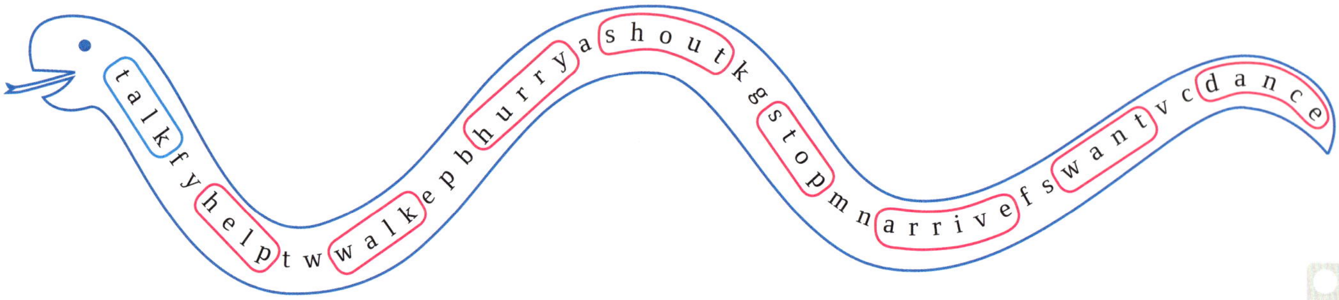

talked, helped, walked, hurried, shouted, stopped, arrived, wanted, danced

6 PRONUNCIATION What can you hear? ➜ SB (p. 100)

WB 64 Listen to the -ed-sounds. What can you hear? Write the verbs in the correct list.

[t]	[d]	[ɪd]
asked	*arrived*	*collected*
finished	*scored*	*shouted*
talked	*showed*	*started*
watched	*stayed*	*wanted*

7 Find the sentence (Simple past: regular and irregular verbs) ➜ SB (p. 101)

a) Write the simple past forms of the verbs in the puzzle.
Then finish the sentence with the words in the blue boxes.

1 *ask* · 2 have · 3 jump · 4 win · 5 stay · 6 see · 7 stop · 8 come · 9 hurry · 10 go · 11 score

Before the match, *Sam was excited.*

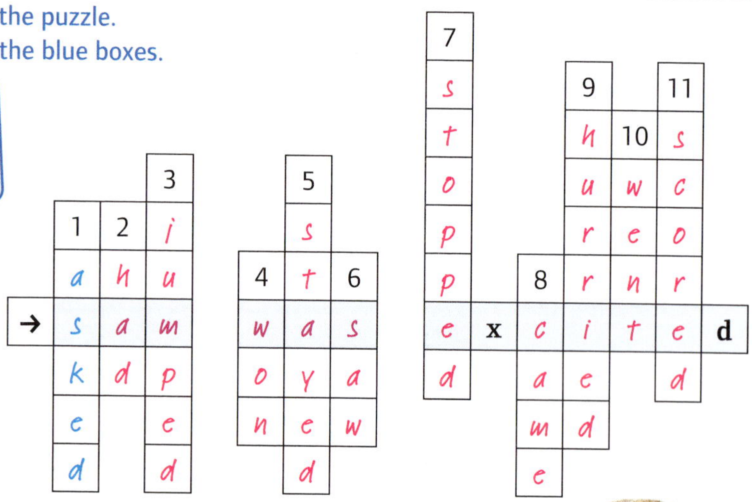

b) Finish what Sam says with words from a).

On Saturday we *had* a big match in Devonport. Our team *went* there by minibus. Lots of fans *came* too. In the last minute of the second half we *stopped* Devonport's best player. I *scored* and our team *won* the match. Our trainer *jumped* up and down like a madman!

8 Nina's diary ➔ SB (p. 101)

a) Read the text. Are the sentences 1–9 right or wrong? Circle the correct letters.

Dear Diary,
Last Saturday was fantastic! We had a big party and all our friends came. In the morning we were busy. I made pizza and we took the food to Dan's house because the party was in his garden. Charlotte made lots of sandwiches. There was Emily's chocolate dessert too. Yummy! And Dan's biscuits were great. The party started at about 3 o'clock – and finished late!
We had a cool time. First we played football with Charlie, Dan's dog. He ran away with some food – he loved the meat sandwiches and my salami pizza. We all shouted and ran after him, so he jumped over the wall[1] into the next garden – not good for the vegetables …
Later we had a music quiz, boys against girls. Guess who won! The girls, of course!
In the evening we played some cool CDs and danced. Charlie ran round the garden and barked to the music – it was very loud. Charlie had my new sunglasses on, and Amira's new sun hat. He looked so cool and he was excited. We had lots of fun with him. The video of the party was great. Charlie was the big star! He can come to our next party!

		Right	Wrong
1	All the kids' friends came to the party.	**E**	A
2	Emily made pizza.	M	**R**
3	The party was at Dan's house.	**A**	S
4	Dan made sandwiches.	I	**O**
5	The party started at lunchtime.	A	**C**
6	Charlie liked the party food.	**T**	R
7	The boys won the music quiz.	R	**L**
8	The party was quiet.	E	**H**
9	Charlie had lots of fun.	**T**	S

b) Who made the video? In the right order, the correct letters give you a name.

→ It was C h a r l o t t e.

9 Sam didn't do it (Simple past: negative sentences) ➔ SB (p. 103)

Correct these wrong statements about Sam.

1 Sam forgot his French homework. Wrong. He didn't forget his French homework.

2 He had ice cream for lunch. Wrong. He didn't have ice cream for lunch.

3 He ate Lucy's chocolate. Wrong. He didn't eat Lucy's chocolate.

4 He read a magazine in maths. Wrong. He didn't read a magazine in maths.

5 He told silly jokes in history. Wrong. He didn't tell silly jokes in history.

[1] wall [wɔːl] *Mauer*

10 At the Hoe (Simple past: negative sentences) ➜ SB (p. 103)

○ Finish the sentences with a negative verb in the simple past.

1 Lucy had her birthday party on the Hoe this year. She *didn't have* it at home.

2 Abby came on the bus. *She didn't come* on her bike.

3 The kids *didn't go* up Smeaton's Tower. They went on the Wheel.

4 On the Wheel Sam *didn't feel* good. He felt sick.

5 The kids saw the Barbican and the Harbour from the Wheel, but Sam *didn't see* any sights.

6 Four kids liked the ride on the Wheel, but Sam *didn't like* it.

7 After the ride, four kids ran to the picnic, but Sam *didn't run* .

11 Last weekend (Simple past: positive and negative sentences) ➜ SB (p. 103)

Finish the sentences with a positive (+) or a negative (–) verb form.

Last weekend Morph cleaned his bookshelves.

1 Justin *cleaned* (+) his bike. He *didn't clean* (–) his room. (clean)

2 Maya *visited* (+) Abby. She *didn't visit* (–) her uncle. (visit)

3 Sam *didn't go* (–) to the pool. He *went* (+) to his kung fu lesson. (go)

4 Abby *helped* (+) in the kitchen. She *didn't help* (–) in the garden. (help)

5 Charlotte *had* (+) football training. She *didn't have* (–) a match. (have)

6 Abby *didn't go* (–) sailing. She *went* (+) shopping. (go)

7 Nina and Pippa *didn't watch* (–) TV. They *watched* (+) a funny DVD. (watch)

8 Lucy and Maya *rode* (+) their bikes to the park. They *didn't ride* (–) their bikes into town. (ride)

12 Sam's day (Simple past: positive and negative sentences) ➜ SB (p. 103)

● Read about Lucy's party on pp. 102 of your student's book again. Imagine you are Sam. Write an email to a friend about your day.
In your exercise book, write six to eight sentences about the basketball match, the ride on the wheel and the party. Use verbs from the box in the simple past, positive or negative form.

be · eat · go · like · look out · play · ride · run · see · think · win

Yesterday was a great day. In the morning, our basketball team went to ...

13 Lucy's birthday (Simple past: positive and negative sentences) ➜ SB (p. 103)

Finish Lucy's diary text. Use the verbs from the box (positive and negative: –) in the simple past.

Dear Diary,

Today *was* my birthday party – great! I *didn't have* the party at home this year. Maya, Justin and Sam *came* to the Hoe! Abby *arrived* late because she *missed* the bus. We *went* on the Wheel. We *saw* all the sights, but I *didn't see* our school (but the school isn't a sight!) The boats in the harbour *were* really small. Only Sam *didn't look* down. After the ride we *ran* over to the picnic. Dad *wanted* to hear about our ride, so we *sat* down on the grass. Only Sam *didn't run*. He *didn't like* it and he *didn't look* happy. Our picnic was cool. Sam *didn't eat* much. But Sam's team *won* the basketball match against Devonport today, so he *wasn't* sad for long.

be · have (–)
come
arrive · miss
go · see
see (–)
be
look (–) · run
want
sit · run (–)
like (–) · look (–)
eat (–)
win
be (–)

14 Pronunciation course [p/b, t/d, k/g] ➜ SB (p. 105)

a) WB 65 Listen and say these words. Is there a [t]- or a [d]-sound at the end? Write the words in the correct list:

[t]: *worked, note, helped, watched, hurt*

[d]: *told, had, fed, sand, understand*

b) WB 66 Now listen and say these words. Then write them in the correct list:

[p]: *stop, jump, shop*

[k]: *joke, black, cake*

[b]: *job, club, crab*

[g]: *big, bag, leg, pig*

c) WB 67 Practise these statements and Yes/No questions.
Remember, your voice must go up or down at the end. Then listen and check.

1 Holly goes to the Computer Games Club.
2 Does she like it?
3 Was Abby late for the party?
4 Yes, she was. She missed the bus.
5 Justin goes to the Film Making Club.
6 He learns how to edit films there.
7 Can he do it ? Yes, he can.
8 Do all the kids like their clubs? Yes, they do.

15 Weekend activities ➜ SB (pp. 106–107)

What is it about? Choose and write the correct titles.

A visit to a museum — A family evening — A sports match — A weekend in London — A picnic — Saturday shopping

1 *Saturday shopping*

I think the Broadway or Drake Circus in Charles Street are good places to go. You can get everything there – clothes, things for school, CDs and DVDs, sports things and of course lots of things to eat. It's nice just to look round there or go for an ice cream. They are open on Sundays too.

2 *A family evening*

The actors were great and the story was very funny. It was exciting too and we were surprised at the end when Will Smith saved the woman. My sister loved it. There were some fantastic action scenes at the end. We all had a good time. After the film Dad took us for a pizza.

3 *A weekend in London*

We stayed with my aunt and uncle. They have a nice flat in Victoria Road, I think. It isn't far from there to all the sights. We saw lots of cool things and places. We saw the Palace, St. Paul's, the parks – everything. We walked a lot. And the shopping is great. I got some cool new trainers in one of the big sports shops on Oxford Street.

4 *A visit to a museum*

My sister didn't want to go, because it's often boring. But we had a great afternoon. I thought the old cars and bikes and planes were really interesting, and there's the Apollo 10 space module. Dad loved that. My sister doesn't like science much, but she said it was great too. We didn't have enough time to see everything.

16 Did you …? (Simple past: questions) ➜ SB (p. 108)

Holly went to visit her friend Jessica in Bath at the weekend. Lucy had lots of questions.
Use the notes to write Lucy's questions.

1 (you – have a good time) *Did you have a good time?*

2 (Jessica – show you the city) *Did Jessica show you the city?*

3 (you – get up early) *Did you get up early?*

4 (you – meet Jessica's friends) *Did you meet Jessica's friends?*

5 (you - like her brother) *Did you like her brother?*

6 (he – like you) *Did he like you?*

7 (you and Jessica – go shopping) *Did you and Jessica go shopping?*

8 (you – buy me a present) *Did you buy me a present?*

17 What did you do today? (Simple past: questions with question words) ➜ SB (p. 108)

Lucy's mum asked Lucy about her day at school. Write her questions. She wanted to know:

1 … what subjects Lucy had. *What subjects did you have?*

2 … what she had for lunch. *What did you have for lunch?*

3 … where she went after school. *Where did you go after school?*

4 … who she met there. *Who did you meet there?*

5 … what she did there. *What did you do there?*

6 … what she bought. *What did you buy?*

18 Ask Maya (Simple past: questions) ➜ SB (p. 108)

Read Maya's answers. Then write your questions with Did …? or with a question word + did …?

what · when · where · who

1 *Did you* go sailing last Sunday, Maya?	Yes, I did.
2 *Who did you take* with you?	I took Abby and her brother Tim with me.
3 *Where did you* go?	We went to Ivy Island.
4 *Did you* see any seals?	Yes, we did.
5 *Where did you* see the seals?	We saw them on the beach.
6 *Did they* follow you?	Yes, they did. It was scary.
7 *What did you* do?	Nothing. We were quiet and we waited.
8 *When did you* get back home?	Late. At about seven o'clock.

19 Not a good weekend ➜ SB (p. 108)

a) WB 68 Read the statements 1–6 first. Then listen to Nina and Dan and (circle) the correct letters.

1 Nina went to town on (N) Saturday morning./ B Saturday afternoon.

2 She met a friend and they went for A a cup of tea./(C) an ice cream.

3 When she left the café, she forgot her (I) bag./ G umbrella.

4 On Saturday afternoon, Dan and his friend went C skating./(I) riding.

5 On Sunday he (P) watched a DVD./ S went to the cinema.

6 After the weekend Nina had no bag, no money, no mobile and no M ring./(C) watch.

b) What did Nina and Amira take with them on their bike ride to the lake? Put the letters before your answers in a) in the correct order.

➜ They took a *p i c n i c* with them.

20 You mustn't be late (*must, needn't, mustn't*) ➔ SB (p. 109)

Lucy and Holly want to visit their grandparents on the farm. Complete with **must**, **needn't** or **mustn't**.

Mum: You *mustn't* be late for the bus. It leaves at 8:15 so you *must* get up early. You can have a good breakfast, so you *needn't* take sandwiches. And Holly, you *mustn't* stay in bed till lunchtime on Sunday. You *must* get up early and help on the farm. You *needn't* wake up at 6 o'clock, but you *must* help Grandpa with the animals. The problem is that you go to bed too late. You *mustn't* watch DVDs till midnight on Saturday.

Holly: OK, Mum, you *needn't* worry. Lucy helps Grandpa on the farm and I always help Grandma in the kitchen.

21 Signs (*must, needn't, mustn't*) ➔ SB (p. 109)

You are in town with your English visitors. Tell them what the signs say. Use **must**, **needn't** or **mustn't**.

1

2

3

4

5

6

7

8

1 *It says that you must leave your bags here.*

2 … you *mustn't use your mobile.*

3 … you *must show your ticket.*

4 … you *mustn't play loud music.*

5 … you *needn't wait for your food.*

6 … dogs *must stay outside.*

7 … children 12 and under *needn't pay.*

8 … you *mustn't leave your bike here.*

22 A visit to the zoo ➔ SB (p. 109)

Your English visitors would like to go to the zoo. Find the information on the poster and answer their questions in English in your own words.

Bestaunen Sie ca. 2 000 Tiere in schönen, artgerechten Gehegen. Verbringen Sie den Tag mit Bären, Giraffen, Zebras, Nashörnern, Elefanten, Großkatzen, Pavianen, Schimpansen, Seehunden, Reptilien, Papageien u. v. m.

Gehen Sie bei einer **Führung** mit. Führungen finden dreimal täglich statt: 10:30, 13:00 und 16:00 Uhr. Treffpunkt ist der Pavillon am Eingang. Erfahrene Tierpfleger beantworten Ihre Fragen und erzählen lustige und spannende Geschichten aus dem Zooalltag. Im Sommer finden auch Abendführungen statt.

Oder schauen Sie bei einer Fütterung zu. Im Interesse der Tiere werden Zoobesucher jedoch gebeten, kein Futter für die Tiere mitzubringen. An den Automaten können Sie preiswert geeignetes Futter käuflich erwerben.

Fütterungszeiten
Seehunde: täglich 14:00 und 15:30
Pelikane: 14:30
Aktuelle Informationen zu weiteren Fütterungszeiten erhalten Sie an der Kasse.

Öffnungszeiten
täglich 9:00–18:30
(Sommer)

1 What animals can you see there?
2 Can you feed the animals?
3 We like seals. When is their feeding time?
4 What time are the tours?
5 Can you ask questions?
6 When does the zoo open?

23 MIXED BAG At Grandma's farm ➔ SB (p. 109)

Lucy and Holly visited their grandparents on the farm. Maya asks Lucy about their weekend. Complete the dialogue. Use verbs in the simple present or simple past.

Lucy: We always *go* to Dartmoor by bus. When we *arrive* at the farm, Grandma *makes* us tea and biscuits. We often *talk* about school and friends. After that Grandpa *takes* us to see the animals.

Maya: *Did* you feed the animals again with your Grandpa yesterday?

Lucy: Yes, *I did*. I *got up* at 6 o'clock on Sunday morning. I *fed* the pigs first, then the rabbits.

Maya: And Holly? *Did* she help with the pigs?

Lucy: No, she never *helps* with the pigs. She usually *stays* in the house and *makes* lunch with Grandma.

Maya: Well, did she *help* with the other animals yesterday, with the horses or the rabbits?

Lucy: No, she *didn't*. She *doesn't* like farms much. Last year, at breakfast one Sunday, a little mouse *came* into the kitchen. Holly *saw* it and *jumped* on her chair. She *shouted* 'Help! Help!' I *said* 'Holly, it's a little mouse, not a big lion!' But Holly *didn't* think that *was* funny.

24 STUDY SKILLS Putting a page together ➜ SB (p. 110)

a) ● Put the parts of Dan's story in the right order. Write 1–4 in the boxes.

[3] Suddenly Charlie ran up a hill and I followed him. But his ball rolled down the hill on the other side and Charlie ran after it. And near the red ball I saw a big, angry bull[1] … Charlie was just one metre from the ball – and from the bull. Charlie was in trouble. It was so scary. I just watched and waited and hoped … Then suddenly the bull turned around and walked away. Charlie ran up the hill with his ball – and I gave[2] him a big, long hug …

[2] On Sunday we went to Dartmoor. First we saw a farm with lots of animals. Charlie barked a lot. After that we played Charlie's game. He runs away with his ball and I run after him.

[4] I didn't tell Mum and Dad about the bull. It was our secret[3].

[1] We live in a city, so at the weekend we often go to the country[4] with Charlie.

b) Make a page for your My Book. Choose a title for the story or write your own title. Write the text in the right order.

An exciting day | Charlie in trouble | A walk to remember

c) Draw one or two pictures from the story and give your pictures captions.

d) Arrange the text, your pictures and your captions on your page.

25 One Saturday afternoon ➜ SB (p. 110)

Put the missing sentences A–F in the right place. Write a letter in each box.

One Saturday afternoon, Lucy and Maya went to the Broadway. They didn't have much money, so they just looked in the shops. [D] They went to a café for a drink. They sat at a table in the corner. At one table there was an old man with a paper. [C]

People came and went. After ten minutes the old man and his dog went too. The paper was still on the table. "Hey, there's a Devon News. Let's look at the TV programme for this weekend," said Lucy. "Good idea," said Maya. She went over to the table, took the paper – and saw a mobile phone on the floor. "Oh, look, Luce," she said. "There's a mobile. Maybe the old man didn't see it because his dog was under the table. Maybe we can find him and give him his mobile back. Let's go."

There were lots of people in the street. [B] "Too late," said Maya. "And his mobile? Maybe he needs it." Then suddenly Lucy said, "Look! There's a man with a dog. Hurry up! [F]" The girls ran up the street. "Hello. [A] We think this is your mobile phone. It was on the floor under the table. You forgot it," said Maya to the old man. "But my mobile is here. Look!" he answered with a smile. The girls looked surprised. "It isn't your mobile? Oh no! Then we're thieves! Come on, Luce [E] – and we have to run!"

A You were in the Broadway café, right?
B The girls couldn't see the old man.
C He had his dog with him too.
D It was hot in the shopping mall and they were thirsty.
E We have to take it back to the café.
F I think that's him!

[1]bull [bʊl] *Stier* [2]gave [geɪv] *gab* [3]secret ['siːkrət] *Geheimnis* [4]to the country *aufs Land*

26 TEXT A baby seal → SB (pp. 112–113)

a) ○ Read pp. 112–113 of your student's book again. Write the missing words.
In the correct order, the letters in the blue boxes give you a place name. What is it?

1 The baby seal had b r i g h t eyes.

2 The baby seal m o v e d over the sand to a pool of water.

3 The little seal was h u n g r y because she couldn't drink her mother's milk.

4 Abby was too young to s t e e r the boat.

5 The boat h i t the rocks because Tim was too slow.

6 Seals can bite, so you have to be c a r e f u l .

7 A baby seal can d i e without milk.

8 The rescue team put the baby seal in a c a g e .

9 The seal didn't get e n o u g h milk from her mother.

→ The place name is I v y I s l a n d .

b) Put the sentences in the correct order of the story. Write 1–8 in the boxes.

- [6] Abby ran to the baby seal.
- [1] A baby seal with bright eyes drank her mother's milk.
- [8] Abby called the baby seal Silky.
- [3] Abby saw something white on the beach.
- [4] Tim, Abby and Will sailed back to the beach.
- [2] At the end of the day the seal couldn't find her mother.
- [7] The rescue team arrived.
- [5] The boat hit the rocks and threw Will into the water.

c) ● Tell the story in 6–8 short sentences. Use simple past verb forms.

d) ● Do you like the story? Why or why not? Write two or more sentences.

I like/don't like the story because ...

1 WORDS Understanding new words

a) Look at the pictures. Then read the text.

Welcome to Woodlands Theme Park

A fun day for all the family – from beginning to end!

Visit many indoor and outdoor centres!
You love excitement? Then choose from over 16 rides and attractions in different zones.
Visit the Falcon Centre! Learn about these wonderful birds. Visit the Reptile House or the Deer Park.
Meet dinosaurs and look for dinosaur eggs on the Dinosaur Farm Ride.

b) Do you understand the underlined words? Write them in the lists 1–3.

1 The pictures help with these words: falcon, deer

2 Like German words: theme park, beginning, (falcon), attractions, wonderful, reptile, dinosaurs

3 I know part of these words: indoor, outdoor, excitement

2 Nick was sick

Use the simple past of the verbs in brackets ( ). Write positive and negative forms.

Nick was (be) sick so he didn't go (go) to school. He thought (think) it was cool – a day in bed. He listened (listen) to his MP3 player, but his mum took (take) it away. He had to (have to) sleep. He didn't watch (watch) TV because it was boring. His magazines were (be) all old. His friends didn't visit (visit) him after school because they went (go) to the shops. In the evening he said (say), "Mum, can I go to school again? Please?"

3 Weekend activities

What is it about? Which title is the best? Match and write a letter (A–E) in the boxes.

1 It started at three o'clock. Our friends and parents came to watch, teachers too. I thought maybe we could win. Jamie is our best player, but he didn't score in the first half. But in the second half he made lots of baskets. So we won the trophy! [E]

2 It's a long way. We can walk or take our bikes. Don't forget a football and something to sit on. We can put the sandwiches, the salad, the cake and the fruit in one basket and the drinks in the other basket. Can we fish in the river? [C]

3 It was a hot day, but it was cool at the lake. We stopped there for a drink and we ate our sandwiches. We left our bikes near the trees. I think we rode about one hour, not too far, but we were tired in the evening. We all had a good time. [A]

A A bike tour **B** A football match **C** A picnic near the river **D** Party food **E** A basketball match

4 Abby's favourite sport

a) Read what Abby says about sailing. Underline new words and try to understand them.

In our family we all like sport. I love sailing. Will is the best sailor of us children, but Tim thinks *he's* the best. Mum started sailing when she was at university in Plymouth. Mum does gymnastics every Thursday too. Dad learned how to sail from his dad, Grandpa Blackwell, when he was about seven. Grandpa often took him out in his boat. Dad said it was really scary when the waves were high and he was cold, but he didn't tell Grandpa. Dad goes to basketball on Tuesdays too, but sailing is his favourite. I have a trophy, but Dad has six. When you live near the sea, sailing is often part of your life.

There are lots of sailing clubs in and around Plymouth. At our club in Wembury everybody is friendly and there are lots of kids.

We don't have a boat. The club has a big boat park on the beach, so you don't need a boat. But you have to be a good swimmer. I took a sailing course because there's a lot to learn. You have to know the different types of boats, the names of the parts of a boat, and about the sails. You have to learn how to leave the harbour, how to stop, how to turn. My teacher was Ben Ashley, Dad's friend. He helped me a lot.

In August 2012 we travelled to Weymouth, where the Olympic sailing was. It isn't far from Plymouth. We watched the best sailors in the world. Ben Ainslie, Dad's favourite, won his fourth gold medal. Wow! He was so cool and it was so exciting! Sailing isn't easy, so you have to practise for years.

b) Are the sentences right (✓) or wrong (✗)?

1 Abby's brother Tim sails best. ✗
2 Abby's mum learned sailing at university. ✓
3 Abby's dad learned sailing from his father. ✓
4 He was only seven years old. ✓
5 Abby's dad plays basketball on Thursdays. ✗
6 Mr Blackwell has some sailing trophies. ✓
7 There aren't many sailing clubs in Plymouth. ✗
8 Abby's sailing teacher was Ben Ainslie. ✗

c) Answer the questions in one or two sentences.

1 What do you have to learn before you can sail? *You have to know the names of the parts of a boat. You have to learn how to leave the harbour, how to stop and how to turn your boat.*

2 Why was August 2012 exciting for the Blackwells? *They watched the sailing in Weymouth. Ben Ainslie won gold.*

Check: Reading

a) Vergleiche deine Antworten mit den Lösungen auf Seite 84 im Workbook.
b) Schätze dann deine Antworten mit einem grünen oder roten Gesicht ein.

	☺	☹	
1 WORDS Understanding new words Konntest du die unterstrichenen Wörter verstehen und den Listen zuordnen?	○	○	→ 1, 3b
3 Weekend activities Konntest du die Titel den Texten richtig zuordnen?	○	○	→ 2
4 Abby's favourite sport 1 Konntest du die Sätze in 4b) ohne Probleme zuordnen?	○	○	→ 3c
2 Konntest du die Fragen in 4c) richtig beantworten?	○	○	→ 3d

c) Wenn du dich rot eingeschätzt hast, schau dir die rechte Spalte an. Die Nummern führen dich zu den passenden Übungen im Skills Training (S. 68–69). Dort kannst du gezielt Leseverstehen trainieren.

1 Grey seals

a) Read the text. Do you understand the underlined words?

Over a third of the world's grey seals live in British waters. People think there are over 180,000 of them. You can often see them up and down the rocky coast of the south-west counties, Devon and Cornwall, but there are many more, about 90 per cent, on the coast and islands of Scotland. Grey seals spend most of their time in water, but they like to sit in the sun on the rocks or on sandy beaches. When the weather is windy and stormy, seals are in trouble. They are sometimes hurt because the high waves throw them against the rocks.

TIP: Before you read the text, look at the **title** and **pictures**. Read the text two or three times.

TIP: You don't have to understand every new word. You can often **guess** a new word from the words before and after it. What do you think 'waves' are?

b) Put the underlined words from a) into two groups.

1 Some words are like German words. Find four or more.

world, south-west, per cent, coast, Scotland, weather, windy, stormy, (sandy)

2 Some words are like other English words, or you know part of the English word. Find three.

a third, rocky, sandy, (stormy)

2 What is it about?

What are the text parts about? Write the letters A–F in the correct boxes.

A We can 'sing' too! We are very loud. We are sometimes 30 metres long and we can weigh 45 tons! In winter we swim to warm places. We usually travel in groups. People love to watch us and take photos!

B Life on the beach isn't always good. We have a hard shell, but big sea animals like to eat us. People like to catch us in nets and eat us in salads or sandwiches. What are we?

C We swim most of the time, but we like to sit in the sun too. We can live for 30 years or more. Our babies are white, soft and very nice.

D We are very, very big. We can swim over 30 miles in an hour, but we aren't fish. We give milk to our babies. We can stay under water only for about 35 minutes. Then we have to swim up because we need air.

E We are big and we are excellent swimmers. We can swim 70 metres down into the sea for food. We can weigh over 200 kilos and adults are over 2 metres long.

F We spend our time on the beach in the wet sand, under rocks or in the water. We are small, sometimes very small. But be careful, we can bite you!

C, E

B, F

A, D

3 Devon's national park

a) Read the text about Dartmoor.

Every year there are <u>thousands</u> of <u>visitors</u> to Dartmoor. It has <u>miles</u> of open countryside, hills, rivers, trees and rocks and lots of things to do. Favourite activities are walking and <u>biking</u>, but <u>hill-climbing</u>, horse-riding or watching birds and animals are also <u>popular</u>. You can see sheep, cows, horses, <u>colourful</u> butterflies and birds. Everybody loves the Dartmoor <u>ponies</u>. You find them in lots of places. But be careful. Don't feed or <u>stroke</u> them. They can bite.

More sport? You can steer your <u>canoe</u> down the River Dart, swim or <u>fish</u>. <u>Fly</u> your <u>kite</u> on the <u>windy</u> hills or visit old castles and <u>ruins</u>. Have a picnic by the river too!

Why not stay <u>overnight</u>? <u>Camping</u> is popular in summer. You can stay the night on a farm too. Dartmoor farms <u>serve</u> a great breakfast or cream tea. Children are very welcome. They can often <u>stroke</u> the animals and help to feed the rabbits and chickens.

Just one more thing: on your Dartmoor walking tours you need warm clothes, good shoes, food and water – and a very good map.

b) Think about what helps you to understand the <u>underlined</u> words. Then write four or five words in each list.

The pictures help with these words:	These words are like German words:	I know a part of these words:
stroke, fly, kite, camping	*thousands, miles, popular,*	*visitors, biking, hill-climbing,*
	ponies, canoe, fish, windy,	*colourful, (windy), overnight*
	ruins, (camping), serve	

c) Are the sentences right (✓) or wrong (✗)?

1 Dartmoor National Park is in Devon. ✓
2 On Dartmoor, most people like walking and biking. ✓
3 You can see lots of ponies on Dartmoor. ✓
4 You can feed the ponies. ✗
5 You can't swim or fish on Dartmoor. ✗
6 People can't stay on the farms. ✗
7 Children can often feed farm animals. ✓
8 You don't need warm clothes. ✗

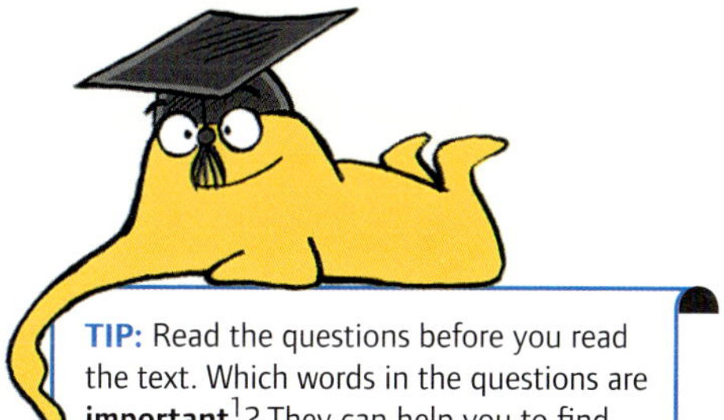

TIP: Read the questions before you read the text. Which words in the questions are **important**[1]? They can help you to find the answers.

d) Answer the questions.

1 What activities can you do on Dartmoor? – You can *walk, ride a bike, ride a horse, watch birds and animals.*

2 What animals can you see on Dartmoor? – *You can see horses, butterflies, birds, ponies.*

[1] important [ɪm'pɔːtənt] *wichtig*

By the sea

The ferry crossing

1 Cawsand Beach ➜ SB (pp. 120–121)

a) Read what Dan says about Cawsand Beach.

From Plymouth it isn't far to Cawsand Beach. People from Plymouth often go there on warm, sunny days. In the summer holidays there are lots of visitors to the beach because it's very popular with families. Cawsand isn't in Devon. It's in Cornwall, the next county. Cornwall has lots of fantastic beaches, but we like Cawsand because it isn't far for an afternoon and it's easy to get there. You can go there by car or bus. It's about 24 miles away. But there's also a ferry crossing from the Barbican. The ferry is nice on a warm day. You can see seals in the Sound, sometimes dolphins, and always lots of colourful boats. The crossing only takes about 30 minutes. People from Plymouth call the ferry boat the Red Pig. I really don't know why.

Cawsand Beach

Cawsand Beach isn't big, but it's clean and great for kids. You can often see seals on the rocks and you can look for crabs in the rock pools. You can swim, go sailing or windsurfing, play ball games or have a picnic. There are cafés, restaurants and small shops too where they sell great ice cream. We usually go to Cawsand by ferry. We sometimes take Charlie. He loves boats. He always barks at the seagulls and wants to catch them. But people don't like dogs on the beach in summer, so Dad takes him for a long walk and meets us at the ferry when it's time to go home. Charlie loves to run up and down the rocks and bark at the crabs and seals. Last year a big crab pinched his nose. Poor Charlie! Now he's careful because crabs aren't his friends.

b) Are the sentences right or wrong? Circle a letter.

	Right	Wrong
1 Cawsand is a good beach for families.	**U**	B
2 Cawsand is in Devon.	B	**U**
3 You can only get to Cawsand Beach by ferry.	R	**A**
4 The ferry leaves from the Barbican.	**A**	I
5 People in Plymouth call the ferry boat the Red Dog.	C	**Q**
6 Charlie barks because he doesn't like to go on boats.	N	**M**
7 Dogs are not welcome on Cawsand Beach in summer.	**I**	R
8 Charlie doesn't like crabs.	**R**	N

c) In the right order, the correct letters give you the name of an interesting place in Plymouth.

➜ It's the A q u a r i u m .

2 Help Morph! (*-ing* forms) ➜ *SB (p. 124)*

Write the -ing forms in three lists.

come · eat · get · have · hit · make · miss · move · run · stop · swim · take · wait · watch · wear

call → calling	sit → sitting	write → writing
eat – eating	*get – getting*	*come – coming*
miss – missing	*hit – hitting*	*have – having*
wait – waiting	*run – running*	*make – making*
watch – watching	*stop – stopping*	*move – moving*
wear – wearing	*swim – swimming*	*take – taking*

3 On the beach (Present progressive: positive sentences) ➜ *SB (p. 124)*

Write about the people in the picture. What are they doing?
Use the words in the box with verbs in the present progressive.

write a postcard[1] · *look for crabs* · eat sandwiches · watch Amira · swim · run after a ball · sit on the rocks · wait for food · film the seals · have an ice cream

1 Charlie *is looking for crabs.*

2 Amira *is swimming.*

3 Emily *is watching Amira.*

4 Dan and Nick *are eating sandwiches.*

5 Two seagulls *are waiting for food.*

6 Nina *is writing a postcard.*

7 Two seals *are sitting on the rocks.*

8 Charlotte *is filming the seals.*

9 A girl *is having an ice cream.*

10 Two boys *are running after a ball.*

[1] postcard ['pəʊstkɑːd] *Ansichtskarte*

4 Nina's postcard[1] ➜ SB (p. 124)

Look at the picture in exercise 3 on p. 71 again. Nina is writing a postcard[1] to a friend.
Imagine you are Nina. Write her postcard. Write five or more sentences in your exercise book.
Use verbs in the present progressive.

Hi, Amy!

I'm sitting on Cawsand Beach in the sun. I'm watching my friend Amira. She …

____

____

____

Bye! Nina

5 Abby's email (Present progressive: negative statements) ➜ SB (p. 125)

Today is not a good day for the beach.
Finish Abby's email with negative verb forms in the present progressive.
Choose verbs from the box. There are more than you need.

bark · drink · have · laugh · play · read · run · sit · speak · swim · take · watch

Today is wet, so we *aren't having* a picnic on the beach. I*'m not sitting* in the sun and Tim and his friends *aren't swimming* because the water is too cold. Dad and Will *aren't playing* football and Mum *isn't reading* her book. Skip *isn't running* on the beach either, so the seals are happy because he *isn't barking* at them today!

6 But not today (Simple present and present progressive) ➜ SB (p. 125)

Finish the text with verbs in the simple present or present progressive.

Sam usually *gets up* (get up) at half past seven. Every day he *has* (have) cornflakes for breakfast, *takes* (take) his school bag and *walks* (walk) to school. But not today.
He *isn't wearing* (not wear) his uniform and he *isn't going* (not go) to school.
At the moment he*'s running* (run) on the beach with his friends. He*'s telling* (tell) silly jokes and all the kids *are laughing* (laugh). Lucy *is eating* (eat) an ice cream and Maya *is taking* (take) photos. Now they*'re sitting* (sit) on a big rock.
They*'re having* (have) a snack and Justin *is filming* (film) the seals.
Sam*'s having* (have) a great time. Suddenly a loud voice from downstairs *shouts* (shout), "Sam, time to wake up. Don't be late for school! It's a cold, wet day."

[1] postcard ['pəʊstkɑːd] *Ansichtskarte*

7 Sam's text ➜ SB (p. 127)

You are in Plymouth with your school class. Sam texts you.

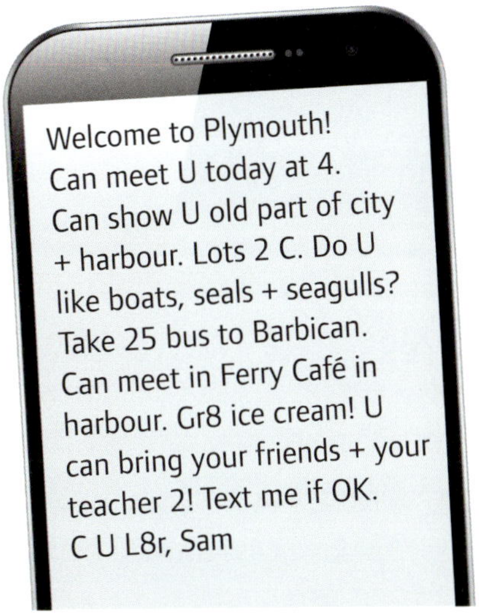

a) Read Sam's text out loud. What does it say?

U = you

\+ = and

2 = to and too

C = see

Gr8 = great

C U L8r = See you later

b) Tell your friends in German what Sam wrote.

Er schreibt, dass ...

Er fragt/möchte wissen, ob ...

Wir sollen ... Er kann ...

Ich soll ihm mitteilen, ...

8 Two phone calls (Present progressive: questions) ➜ SB (p. 128)

a) Nick calls Dan. Finish their dialogue with questions in the present progressive and short answers.

Nick: Hi, Dan! What are you doing (do)? Are you playing (play) computer games?

Dan: No, I'm not. Not today.

Nick: Oh, well, what is your sister doing (do)? Is she watching (watch) that new DVD?

Dan: Yes, she is. It's really funny. Two of her friends are here too.

Nick: Oh, really? That sounds great. Are they laughing (laugh) a lot?

Dan: Yes, they are. But why are you asking (ask) all these questions?

What are you doing (do) now?

Nick: Nothing. That's the problem. It's boring. Can I come to your house?

Dan: Yes, great idea! I have to clean my room now. You can help me.

b) ● Tim is playing loud music. He can't hear what Abby is saying. Write his questions. Start with *What* or *Where* and ask about the **red** words.

Abby: Tim, Mum is calling. She**'s shopping**.

Tim: I can't hear you. What is Mum doing?

Abby: She's shopping **at the Broadway**.

Tim: Sorry, where is she shopping?

Abby: At the Broadway! And Dad **is sailing** with Uncle John.

Tim: I can't hear you, Abby. What is Dad doing?

Abby: Oh, Tim! He's sailing with Uncle John **in the Sound**.

Tim: Sorry, but where is he sailing?

Abby: On the water, silly!

9 What's everybody doing? → SB (p. 128)

a) WB 69 Read the sentences, then listen to Dan and Nick. What's right? Underline the letters after your answers.

1. It's Saturday (M) / Sunday (I).
2. Dan is sitting on a bus (A) / in the cinema (C).
3. Dan's cousin John (E) / Jeff (D) is with him.
4. Nick is reading (E) / is sitting in the park (A).
5. Nina and Emily are shopping (G) / are at the Lido (E).
6. Noah is skating (G) / is at the sports centre with Leo (A).
7. Charlotte is riding (E) / is helping her dad (S).
8. Nick's brother is visiting a friend in Cawsand (C) / is swimming on Cawsand Beach (S)
9. The film starts at 2.30 (I) / 3.30 (A).
10. You take the 25 bus (R) / the 52 bus (I) to the Barbican.

b) The letters after the correct answers give you the name of the film Dan and his cousin want to see.

→ The film is M a d a g a s c a r 4.

10 REVISION WORDS Opposites → SB (p. 129)

a) ○ Find and write pairs of opposites.

early – late	exciting – boring	push – pull
arrives – leaves	hard – soft	first – last
fast – slow	good – bad	before – after

b) Finish with word pairs from a).

1. Plymouth is an exciting city with lots to do. It's never boring.
2. The ferry to Cawsand leaves at 10:30 and arrives about 30 minutes later.
3. You can go on the first ferry and come back on the last ferry at half past four.
4. The city tour leaves at 9:30. Don't be late. Come early so we can sit at the front of the bus.
5. The Wheel isn't scary. The ride is slow. It isn't fast.

11 A bike tour (Describing a picture) ➔ SB (p. 129)

Describe the picture. Write in your exercise book. Who can you see? What are they doing? What are they wearing? What can you see where? Use the present progressive and these phrases and prepositions: I can see …, There is/are …, On the right/left …, In the middle/foreground/background …; behind, in front of, near

12 A trip to Nuremberg ➔ SB (p. 129)

Tell an English girl in your class about the class trip to Nuremberg next week. Write in your exercise book.

TIP: Don't translate. Say what is important. Say the places you visit and when.

Klassenfahrt nach Nürnberg: 24.–26. Juni

Dienstag

- Abfahrt Schule (Bus) 9:00
- Ankunft / Mittagessen 12:00
- Stadtrundfahrt mit Führung 14:00
- Abend: Spaziergang Altstadt

Mittwoch

- Besuch Kaiserburg + Museum mit Führung 10:00
- Nachmittag: Spielzeugmuseum oder Schulmuseum (2 Gruppen) 14:00
- Abend: Freizeit im Hostel

Donnerstag

- Albrecht-Dürer-Haus mit Führung 10:00
- Abfahrt nach Mittagessen ca. 14:30

There's a class trip to Nuremberg next week. On Tuesday, we leave school at 9 o'clock and we arrive in Nuremberg at … Then we … In the afternoon, there's …

13 STUDY SKILLS Preparing and giving a mini-talk ➜ SB (p. 132)

Prepare a poster and a mini-talk about the Wheel of Plymouth <u>or</u> a place/sight in your town.
You can use the information on this page and the internet.

a) Make a poster.
The texts on your poster can be short. Choose only important and interesting information.
You can use the other information in your mini-talk.

About the Wheel of Plymouth

- came to Plymouth in 2011
- on Plymouth Hoe, near the water, easy to get there
- 60 metres high
- 42 capsules[1]
- can see over the town and the Sound
- on a good day can see 24 miles
- fantastic at night when it's dark
- the ride is 13 minutes long

- open every day from 10 am to 7 pm (Friday and Saturday till 9 pm)

Ticket prices:
- adult £ 8.50
- child £ 5.50
- family ticket (2 adults, 2 children) £ 20 (only £ 17 online)

Arrange your title and subtitle, your pictures, your picture captions and your texts on your poster.
For ideas look at Sam and Justin's poster again, in your student's book on page 131.
These ideas can help you too:

Your title and subtitle: The Wheel of Plymouth! / My favourite city sight — The Wheel of Plymouth! / Fun for all the family

Your picture captions: A really cool ride — It's so exciting!

b) ● Prepare and practise your mini-talk.
Practise your talk at home. In class show your poster.
Make your talk interesting and easy to understand.
Point to things on your poster. Say what the pictures/drawings show.
You can start like this:

> **TIP:** When you give your talk:
> 1 Look at the class/group.
> 2 Don't read from your poster.
> You can make notes before your talk.
> 3 Speak in a loud voice and don't speak fast.

I'd like to talk about ... because ... Hundreds of tourists ride on ...

It's on Plymouth Hoe, not far from ... The Wheel came ... It's a good idea to ...

You can end your talk like this:

That's the end of my talk. Thanks for listening. Are there any questions?

[1] capsule ['kæpsjuːl] *Gondel*

14 Lucy's photos (Word order) ➔ SB (p. 133)

Finish the sentences with the words in brackets ( ) in the right order.

1 Lucy's favourite place is the Aquarium because … (*exciting sleepovers/can/you/have/there*).

… you can have exciting sleepovers there.

2 The kids watched a 4D film about fish before … (*the aquarium tour/did/they*).

… they did the aquarium tour.

3 Lucy felt excited before … (*in front of/fell asleep/she/the aquarium window*)

… she fell asleep in front of the aquarium window.

4 Lucy didn't want to play cards with Holly because … (*wanted to/she/her talk/work on*).

… she wanted to work on her talk.

5 Lucy looked at her mobile because … (*were/on it/the photos for her talk*)

… the photos for her talk were on it.

6 Lucy wasn't happy when … (*took/her mobile/Holly*).

… Holly took her mobile.

7 Holly laughed when … (*saw/the photos of Lucy and Sam/she*)

… she saw the photos of Lucy and Sam.

15 Weekend shopping (*some* and *any*) ➔ SB (p. 135)

Sam and Lily have to help with the weekend shopping. Complete the dialogue with **some** or **any**.

Sam: Mum's list says that we need some potatoes, some vegetables, cheese and cream.

Lily: I don't like cheese. Let's get some yoghurt. I like yoghurt.

Sam: No, Lily. We don't need any yoghurt today. Please don't touch the yoghurt!

Lily: But we need some chocolate. Do they have any here?

Sam: Maybe, but there isn't any chocolate on Mum's list. We have to buy some cornflakes. Can you see any? Look, I think there are some cornflakes over there, in those big boxes.

Lily: Do they have any toys?

Sam: No, Lily. This isn't a toy shop. There aren't any toys in a food shop. Silly!

Lily: OK. But we need some biscuits. You know, the yummy chocolate biscuits.

Sam: No, Lily. We don't need any biscuits today. There are always some biscuits in the kitchen.

16 Does anybody know …? *(somebody/anybody, something/anything)* ➜ SB (p. 135)

Put in some, any, somebody, anybody, something or anything.

Sam: Does anybody know where my pencil case is? There are some new felt pens in it.

Mum: Your pencil case? Sorry. I don't know anything about it. There aren't any school things in the kitchen. Maybe there are some pencils in the living room. Look there.

Sam: No, Mum. I don't need any pencils. I have to find my new felt pens. I have to do some geography homework and I need them for my maps.

Mum: Mmm. Do your classmates know anything? Text them. Maybe somebody knows something. Call Justin and Lucy. Maybe somebody put your pens in their school bag. No, wait. Just a moment. Is your pencil case red and black, and are there any stickers on it? I saw something red and black in Lily's room. Yes, that's right. In her toy box.

17 MIXED BAG An email to Sam from Ireland ➜ SB (p. 135)

Put in the missing words. If you need a verb, use it from the box in the correct tense (simple present, present progressive, simple past).

arrive · be (4 x) · do · drink · drive · eat · go (2 x) · have (3 x) · hope · look · sit · swim · taste · visit · wait · walk

Hi Sam!

We usually go on holiday to a hot country, but this year we're having a holiday in Ireland. We arrived in Dublin on Saturday. Yesterday morning we did a tour of the city. We visited the castle and other sights. In the afternoon we went to Bull Island by car over a long bridge. Just imagine! You can drive your car on the beach and you can walk for hours on the sand. There are lots of birds and seals too. I watched them when we had our picnic. We always have picnics on a beach. Sand in your sandwiches tastes great!! I swam in the sea too, but the water was too cold. Now I'm sitting in a street café with Dad in the centre of Dublin. We're waiting for Mum and my sister. They're looking at clothes in a big shopping mall. I'm eating my second chocolate ice cream and Dad is drinking his third cup of coffee. Oh, there's Mum now. I can see her, and Sarah too. I can see her red T-shirt – and lots of bags! I hope your holiday is fun too.

Love from us all, Chris

18 Pronunciation course ➜ (p. 137)

a) WB 70 Say the words. Which word has an [əʊ]-sound? Underline it.
Then listen, check and practise.

1 blond – grow – soft
2 lonely – lots – shop
3 copy – coast – bottle
4 song – spoke – chocolate
5 ocean – box – got
6 frog – want – ghost

b) WB 71 Read the dialogue. Where does your voice go up or down at the end?
Write ↗ or ↘ after the sentence. Then listen, check and practise.

Boy: Let's go to the harbour. ↘

Girl: What can we do there? ↘

Boy: We can watch the boats and the seagulls. ↘

Girl: Mmm. Can we get an ice cream? ↗

Boy: Yes, of course. ↘

Girl: How do we get there? ↘

Boy: We can go by bus or we can walk. ↘

Do you like seals? ↗

Girl: Yes, I love seals. ↘

Boy: You can often see some at the harbour. ↘

Girl: Well, let's go! ↘

19 TEXT The pepper smugglers ➜ (pp. 138–139)

a) Read the play in your student's book on pp. 138–139 again.
Finish the sentences with the correct information.

1 Tom White, Jack Hill and Old Bill are at *the Red Lion.*

2 Flynn is Molly's *brother.*

3 Flynn and his friends *are poor now.*

4 A ship from France takes *(bags of) pepper to Cawsand Beach.*

5 Mr Collings knows *about the friends' plans.*

6 Molly hides *in her brother's boat with the boxes for the market.*

7 Molly helps *her brother with a clever idea.*

b) ● In your exercise book, draw a picture of your favourite scene in the story.
The pictures in your student's book can help you.
What's happening in your picture? What are the people doing?
Write three or more sentences in the present progressive.

1 WORDS Cawsand

Finish the text with words from this unit.

Cawsand is a *village* near Plymouth. Two *centuries* ago, it was a great place for *smuggling/smugglers*. The smugglers often *hid* their *goods* in their clothes. Today lots of *tourists* visit Cawsand. The Plymouth kids want to go there by *ferry*. Abby has a new camera. She wants to *take* *photos* of their trip. "I'm hungry. Let's go for a *snack*, maybe a sandwich or an ice cream," says Sam. "No, the food at the café is too *expensive*. I don't have enough money", says Justin, "And it's *almost* 11 o'clock. Look, the boat is coming."

2 About Silky (Simple present or present progressive)

Put in the correct form of the verb in brackets ( ).

On Mondays Silky usually *swims* (swim) to the Hoe, but today she *isn't going* (not, go) there. She *is sitting* (sit) on her rock. At the moment Wilbur *is visiting* (visit) her. They *are having* (have) breakfast. Wilbur *is eating* (eat) lots of Silky's crabs. Oh, no! Now Wilbur *is taking* (take) all the little fish from Silky's plate too! Wilbur always *does* (do) that when he *comes* (come) to her rock for breakfast. Now they *are laughing* (laugh), but Silky has to catch more fish. She *doesn't think* (not, think) it's funny.

3 A visitor from London

Amy is visiting you. She can't speak German and your mum needs help with English.
Tell Amy in English what your mother says and asks. First, mark what is important.

1 Frag Amy bitte, was sie gern zum Frühstück isst. Wir haben Cornflakes, Joghurt, Müsli, frische Semmeln …

Mum asks: what do you have for breakfast?

2 Sag ihr bitte, dass wir normalerweise um 18:30 zu Abend essen. Heute gibt es Braten mit Kartoffeln und Gemüse. Ob sie gern Süßes isst? Frag sie mal. Oder ich mache meinen guten Obstsalat. Den mag ja jeder.

She says that we have dinner at half past six. Do you like dessert? What about a fruit salad?

3 Ich würde gern wissen, wann sie morgens aufsteht. Ich glaube, die Schule fängt in England später an, oder? Sag ihr, dass du schon um 6:30 aufstehen musst. Hoffentlich schafft sie das auch.

Mum asks: when do you get up in the morning? I have to get up at 6:30 am.

4 Frag doch mal, ob sie heute mit dir ins Kino gehen möchte. Ich habe im Kinoprogramm gelesen, dass heute ein lustiger Jugendfilm auf Englisch spielt. Ich habe mir leider nicht gemerkt, wie der Film heißt.

She says that we could go to a cinema today. There's a funny film in English.

4 Signs

Tell your English visitors what these signs say.

1

2

3

5 Learning to sail

You are visiting a Bavarian[1] lake with an English family. 12-year-old Jamie sees this poster.
Read questions 1–8 first. Then read the information on the poster and mark the important words.
Answer the family's questions in English. Write your answers in your exercise book.

Segelschule Schmidt

Herzlich willkommen in unserer traditionsreichen Segelschule!

Informieren Sie sich über unsere Kursprogramme, z. B.:

Einführungskurse (gehen über 3 × 2 Stunden)
Für 2 Personen €260
Familie (2 Erwachsene + 1 Kind) €300
In dieser Woche sind noch wenige Plätze frei.

Kinderprogramm (ab 7 Jahre)
Katamaran-Segelkurse

Jugendprogramm (ab 12 Jahre)
Motorbootkurse, Fortgeschrittenenkurse

Nähere Informationen entnehmen Sie bitte unserem Flyer oder besuchen Sie uns im Schulungshaus.
Unsere erfahrenen Segellehrer/innen geben Ihnen abends von 6–7 Uhr gern Auskunft.

1 Jamie: What's that poster about?
2 Jamie: Are there any courses for beginners[2]?
3 His mum: Which course can Jamie do?
4 Jamie: Can I do a course with mum and dad?
5 His dad: How much is a course for us all?
6 His mum: Can we do a course this week?
7 Jamie: Does it say when the course starts?
8 Mum: How can we find out more?

Check: Mediation

a) Vergleiche deine Antworten mit den Lösungen auf Seite 84 im Workbook.
b) Schätze dann deine Antworten mit einem grünen oder roten Gesicht ein.

	☺	☹	
1 Hast du in Aufgabe 3 die wichtigsten Inhalte erkannt und markiert?	○	○	→ 3
2 Konntest du in Aufgabe 3 kurze Sätze mit eigenen Worten auf Englisch ausdrücken?	○	○	→ 1
3 Konntest du in Aufgabe 4 die Bedeutung der Schilder mit eigenen Worten erklären?	○	○	→ 2
4 Konntest du in Aufgabe 5 die richtigen Informationen zur Beantwortung der Fragen finden und diese mit eigenen Worten auf Englisch ausdrücken?	○	○	→ 3

c) Wenn du dich rot eingeschätzt hast, schau dir die rechte Spalte an. Die Nummern führen dich zu den passenden Übungen im Skills Training (S. 82–83). Dort kannst du gezielt Mediation trainieren.

[1]Bavarian [bəˈveərɪən] *bayerisch* [2]beginner [bɪˈgɪnə] *Anfänger*

1 In town

You are in town with Jamie and a German friend, Timo.
Tell Jamie in English what Timo says or asks.

TIP:
- Use short, easy sentences with words you know.
- You can change words and sentence structure, but use the correct word order.
- You can use these phrases: *X says/asks*

1 Frag ihn, was er nach der Schule und am Wochenende macht.

Timo asks: What do you do in your free time?

2 Er kann heute Nachmittag mit uns Fußball spielen. Sag ihm, was wir machen und frag ihn, ob er dazu Lust hat.

He says: Would you ... like to play football with us after school?

3 Vielleicht interessiert er sich für Geschichte. Wir können mit ihm zu Fuß auf die alte Burg gehen. Oder ins Museum. Frag ihn, ob er so was mag.

Timo asks: Do you like history? We could visit a castle or a museum.

4 Sag ihm, dass wir eine tolle Eisdiele kennen. Sie haben das beste Schokoeis in der ganzen Stadt.

Timo and I know a good place for ice cream. They have the best chocolate ice cream in town.

2 Signs

Read what Jamie asks below.
Then read signs 1–5 and write the answers in your exercise book.

TIP:
- for ‚verboten' use: *we/you can't/mustn't*
- Don't translate. Use different words with the same meaning: z.B. ‚täglich' > *every day*

TIP:
- for signs use *The sign says.../ It says here (that) ...*
- Give only information that answers the question. Leave out extra information (hier: Preise, werktags, Ballmaschine)
- ‚auf Anfrage' > *you/we have to ask*

1

2

3

4

5

Jamie asks:

1 Can we leave our bikes here and walk? No, we can't. It says here ... we mustn't leave them here.

2 That little lake looks nice. Can we swim in it? No, we mustn't swim there.

3 Can we go on the playground[1]? Can your dog go with us? We can go there, but the dog must stay outside.

4 When can we go to the swimming pool? We can go there between 9 am and 6 pm.

5 How about tennis on Saturday? How much is it? And how much is a lesson?

Tennis on Saturday costs €15, we have to ask about the prices for lessons.

[1] playground ['pleɪgraʊnd] *Spielplatz*

3 The Bavarian lakes

You have English visitors. They want to know about the lakes in Bavaria. You find the following information on the internet. Read the questions first and mark the text parts that you need for the answers. Then answer the questions in English.

In Bayern gibt es zwar kein Meer, dafür jedoch über 200 natürliche Seen. Der Chiemsee ist der größte bayerische See mit einer Gesamtfläche von ca. 80 km² und einer Länge von fast 14 km. Wegen seiner Größe wird er sogar ‚bayerisches Meer' genannt. Die drei Inseln im Chiemsee sind mit der Fähre leicht zu erreichen. Auf der Herreninsel befindet sich das Schloss Herrenchiemsee, von König Ludwig II. erbaut. Es ist ein großer Anziehungspunkt für Touristen.

Der Starnberger See ist mit einer Fläche von ca. 56 km² der zweitgrößte See in Bayern. In den beliebten Badeseen, z. B. Chiemsee, Starnberger See oder Tegernsee steigt in den Sommermonaten die Wassertemperatur bis auf 25 °C an. In dem klaren, sauberen Wasser ist das Baden ein Vergnügen.

Weitere beliebte Freizeitaktivitäten am und im Wasser sind Angeln, Wasserski, Surfen, Kite-Surfen, Bootfahren, Tauchen und natürlich Segeln. Auf den größeren Seen werden Schiffsrundfahrten angeboten. Um die Seen gibt es zahlreiche ausgewiesene Wanderwege. Man kann stundenlang wandern oder Rad fahren. Auch erstklassige Campingplätze in malerischer Umgebung ziehen viele Urlauber an. Jedes Jahr kommen immer mehr Besucher aus dem In- und Ausland an die bayerischen Seen.

1 How many lakes are there in Bavaria?

There are more than 200 lakes in Bavaria.

2 Why is the Chiemsee called the 'Bavarian Sea'?

It's called the Bavarian Sea because it's so big.

3 Why is the Chiemsee so popular?

There is a castle on one of the islands.

4 Is the water warm enough for swimming?

Yes, it is.

5 What other water sports can you do?

You can do fishing, water-skiing, surfing, kite-surfing, diving and sailing.

6 What other freetime activities are there?

You can do round trip on a boat, go for walks or ride a bike.

7 Are the Bavarian lakes popular with tourists?

Yes, there are more and more tourists every year.

Checkpoint 1

1 WORDS Don't be late

2 spell 3 timetable 4 trainers 5 wait 6 friends 7 birthday 8 canteen 9 meet 10 exercise book

2 It's big

2 She 3 They 4 He 5 It 6 They

3 An email

2 's/is 3 are 4 are 5 's/is 6 is 7 isn't 8 's/is 9 's/is 10 'm/am 11 aren't 12 're/are 13 Are 14 is 15 am

4 Where are they?

1 D 2 C

5 A party

1 R 2 W 3 R 4 W 5 R 6 W 7 W 8 R 9 R 10 W

Checkpoint 2

1 PRONUNCIATION Food

1 sandwich ['sænwɪtʃ] 2 biscuits ['bɪskɪts] 3 fruit salad [ˌfruːt 'sæləd] 4 dessert [dɪ'zɜːt] 5 vegetables ['vedʒtəblz]

2 WORDS Home and family

a) 1 shelf 2 armchair 3 breakfast 4 uncle 5 divorced
b) 1 play games 2 watch TV 3 do homework 4 write emails 5 feed the dog 6 make a cup of tea 7 read the paper 8 meet friends 9 go sailing
c) **Lösungsvorschlag:** We play games in the break. I usually watch TV on Saturdays. I do my homework after school.

3 About Nick

goes go doesn't have takes likes doesn't like don't like

4 Your dream house

Lösungsvorschlag: 1 My dream house is near the sea/in Germany. 2 It has six rooms and a big swimming pool in the garden. 3 I can swim in my pool every day. 4 My bedroom is upstairs. It's orange and yellow, my favourite colours. It's big and really cool. 5 It has lots of posters and pictures of my family and my dog, and there are lots of shelves for books and games. 6 There's a big TV and a computer in every room.

5 About you

Lösungsvorschlag: We have a nice flat/house in … I have a brother/sister. He's/She's eight years old. My new school is big. I like my classmates and my favourite subject is … I like football/ … and I'm good at basketball/… too. We have a white dog. His name is … I feed him before school. After school, I often go for a walk with him in the park or I go to the shops with a friend.

Checkpoint 3

1 WORDS Can you spell it?

1 skating 2 edit 3 riding 4 guitar 5 drums 6 bike 7 chocolate 8 idea

2 Silky and Morph

1 Does Silky have crabs for breakfast? 2 Where does Silky swim with her friends? 3 Silky doesn't usually swim in the Lido pool. 4 What books does Morph read? 5 Morph often reads stories about ghosts.

3 Plymstock clubs

a) SAMBA – Music area – Mon lunchtime – Mr Willis – dance, sing, play an instrument QUIET READING – Library – Mon to Fri lunchtime – Mr Wood – learn about good books for young people FILM MAKING – TE9 – Thurs 3–4 pm – Mrs Hart – learn to edit videos on the computer
b) **Lösungsvorschlag:** Is lunchtime sometimes boring? Do you like music? Can you sing? Do you dance? Do you know the samba? Come and join our Samba Club – and bring a friend! You can learn a cool dance, sing or play an instrument – and have lots of fun. We meet in the Music area. When? Monday lunchtime.

4 About Leo

a) Age: 12 School: Plymstock Class: 7AG Family: two sisters Animals: a rabbit Arnold Friends: Nina and Nick School subjects: he likes art and science, he doesn't like maths and French. School clubs: Gardening Club and Samba Club Sports: skating, riding his bike Hobbies: he makes model ships, watches TV, plays the drums/guitar Favourite music: hip hop and rap.
b) Leo is 12 years old. He goes to Plymstock School and he's in class 7AG. Leo has two sisters and he has a rabbit. His friends are Nina and Nick. At school his favourite subjects are art and science, but he doesn't like maths or French. He's in the Gardening Club because he likes fruit and vegetables, and he's in the Samba Club because he likes dancing.

Checkpoint 4

1 WORDS Understanding new words

b) 1 falcon, deer 2 theme park, beginning, (falcon), attractions, wonderful, reptile, dinosaurs 3 indoor, outdoor, excitement

2 Nick was sick

was didn't go thought listened took had to didn't watch were didn't visit went said

3 Weekend activities

1 E 2 C 3 A

4 Abby's favourite sport

b) 1 ✗ 2 ✓ 3 ✓ 4 ✓ 5 ✗ 6 ✓ 7 ✗ 8 ✗
c) 1 You have to know the names of the parts of a boat. You have to learn how to leave the harbour, how to stop and how to turn your boat. 2 They watched the sailing in Weymouth. Ben Ainslie won gold.

Checkpoint 5

1 WORDS Cawsand

village centuries smuggling/smugglers hid goods tourists ferry take photos snack expensive almost

2 About Silky

swims isn't going is sitting is visiting are having is eating is taking does comes are laughing doesn't think

3 A visitor from London

1 Mum asks: what do you have for breakfast? 2 She says that we have dinner at half past six. Do you like dessert? What about a fruit salad? 3 Mum asks: when do you get up in the morning? I have to get up at 6:30. 4 She says that we could go to the cinema today. There's a funny film in English.

4 Signs

1 The sign says you mustn't walk on the grass. 2 The sign says you can take a boat on the lake. 3 You can buy small presents here.

5 Learning to sail

1 It's about a sailing school. 2 Yes, there are. 3 He can do a course for teenagers. 4 Yes, there's a course for families. 5 It is 300 euros. 6 Yes, you can. 7 No, it doesn't. 8 You can get information from the teachers between 6 and 7 pm.